THE
kiteboarding
MANUAL

ANDY GRATWICK

THE
kiteboarding
MANUAL

2ND EDITION

The Essential Guide for Beginners and Improvers

ADLARD
COLES

LONDON · OXFORD · NEW YORK · NEW DELHI · SYDNEY

ADLARD COLES
Bloomsbury Publishing Plc
50 Bedford Square, London, WC1B 3DP, UK
29 Earlsfort Terrace, Dublin 2, Ireland

BLOOMSBURY, ADLARD COLES and the Adlard Coles logo are trademarks of
Bloomsbury Publishing Plc

First published 2015
This edition published 2023

British Library Cataloguing-in-Publication Data
A catalogue record for this book is available from the British Library.

Library of Congress Cataloguing-in-Publication data has been applied for.
add where a UK originated single-ISBN edition for which we own US rights

ISBN: 978-1-3994-0129-6
ePDF: 978-1-3994-0127-2
ePub: 978-1-3994-0128-9

2 4 6 8 10 9 7 5 3 1

Typeset in DIN by Gridlock-design
Printed and bound in India by Replika Press Pvt Ltd

FSC
www.fsc.org

MIX
Paper from
responsible sources
FSC® C016779

To find out more about our authors and books visit www.bloomsbury.com
and sign up for our newsletters

Contents

Introduction

It's been almost a decade since I wrote the first edition of this book and a fair bit has happened in the wonderful world of kiteboarding and watersports in general. Stand up paddleboarding (SUP) has exploded since around 2015, with the rise of the inflatable paddleboard enabling hundreds of thousands of people to get afloat on the sea, river, lake or canal. Kiteboarding has become a bona fide Olympic discipline with medals for both women and men in hydrofoil racing. Windsurfing has also become a foiling discipline for Olympic racing. Wingfoiling has taken the world by storm since 2020 as a whole new board sport.

Foiling in general, from the America's Cup and high budget big boat racing, all the way down to prone foiling on a surfboard is booming, everyone wants to float on the ocean and glide silently on the wind and swells. Kiteboarding is experiencing positive growth from this just like many other disciplines, and the showroom of the Olympics will project it front and centre into the mainstream media.

In simple terms, a kiteboarder uses a traction kite to propel themself across water, land or snow on a single-person board, ski or wheeled device. Both the 'engine' (the kite) and the 'wheels' (the board) can take many shapes and forms. Lines and control bars, or sometimes handles, can also differ greatly in length from 10 to 40m (32 to 130ft) with many systems for trimming and safety being available. The sport is governed by the same wind limitations as other sail sports, and follows similar competition rules in racing disciplines. It is possible to achieve great speeds and height in jumps without the need for high winds or big waves.

I am going to guide you through the most common form of the sport, which is kiteboarding on water with a multi-directional or twin-tip board. It should not be used as a way of learning the sport but merely as a form of knowledge-reinforcement; kiteboarding is simply one of those sports that you need to take lessons to learn. Other sports I have mastered, and indeed teach, can be attempted without instruction with limited or no risk if you're sensible, but kiteboarding fits into the same category as piloting cars, planes, helicopters and paragliders. Just like these, it can be safe and lots of fun if practised correctly, but it can be difficult and dangerous if undertaken alone and without structure and guidance.

Let's also make it clear that this book is no substitute for hands-on lessons in any circumstance. Attempting to rig, launch and fly a powerful kiteboarding kite was the source of numerous injuries and worse in the early days, and more guidance than is given here is required. Fortunately those days have passed and there are now safe, structured and affordable lessons available around the globe.

PART 1
Need To Know

The sport:
a brief history

The sport: a brief history

It may be relatively brief by extreme sports' standards, but the history of kiteboarding is as fast-paced and exciting as the sport itself. Truly the product and reflection of a digital age, kiteboarding in all its formats and disciplines has been fortunate to benefit from instant communication, incredible leaps in technology and the fact that you can do something in one part of the globe and immediately share it with people worldwide. These modern advantages have probably accelerated the progression of the sport tenfold in comparison with more mature sports such as surfing, windsurfing or waterskiing. I am not going to try and document, credit or mention every stage in kiteboarding's rich and vibrant history. I will, however, highlight a few important milestones and turning points.

Kiteboarding, as I will call it throughout the book, encompasses all manner of disciplines, but we're looking primarily at on-water riding, which, until recently, was known as kitesurfing. However, there are a number of disciplines that complement, contribute towards and feed into kiteboarding as a whole, namely kite landboarding, kite buggying, snowkiting and the wacky world of kiteboating for propelling multi-person and larger craft.

There is now a mushrooming scene of hydrofoil racing, which is turning the sport professional, with athletes aiming for Olympic stardom with support from their nation's sports structures rather than sponsorship through a specific brand. The watersports world has gone somewhat 'foiling' crazy since around 2017, with every watersport discipline now encompassing foiling in some form, and not just for speed and racing but in freestyle and waves, too.

All of these wonderfully diverse disciplines were bubbling away through the 1980s and early 90s in specific pockets of the world: in the desert flats of Namibia there were land speed assaults and adventures in kite buggies; a project called Jacob's Ladder built catamarans propelled by stacking kites (more on this later); in Oregon, waterskiers zoomed down lakes; and in Europe, French sailors inflated kites to propel surfboards on water. In fact, the sport is so international that there are now invitational camps for kiteboarding entrepreneurs, innovators and athletes from around the globe to discuss and progress business and the sport in new, imaginative ways.

Having watched and lived through kiteboarding's rapid evolution and growth since 1997 I feel proud to have played my small part, and have had such fun travelling

the world and meeting some inspiring people along the way. I have split my account in this chapter into a few historical events that unknowingly formed the basis of the sport, then look at the modern story of kiteboarding, which is still less than 30 years old. This may include the things we remember as sparking our own motivation to get into kiteboarding, from Laird Hamilton's TV footage in Hawaii in the early 2000s to the local heroes displaying their prowess (or maybe not) on the latest brightly coloured kites and boards at a windsurfing beach.

THE EARLY YEARS

So, where do we start? Well, kites have been around for centuries; their use for fun, fighting, propulsion and communication is documented as far back as 2000 years ago. During the intervening years, kites have been involved in some interesting and fairly significant events – from the overthrowing of an emperor to major scientific and engineering feats, as well as annoying English gentry, which is usually a good sign that something is worth pursuing!

In around 200 BC the Chinese general Han Hsin was leader of the rebel army that was fighting against a tyrannical emperor of the time. Han, who was less well-armed than his opponent, is said to have flown kites over the emperor's palace so that he could measure how far his men would have to tunnel in order to breach the palace walls. His plan resulted in victory and the beginning of the 200-year reign of the Western Han dynasty in China. There are also many ancient tales of people being flown and lifted by kites in all sorts of situations, and Chinese history documents great festivals involving kites. These include 'kite fighting', when competitors would fit shards of glass and knives to their lines in an attempt to cut down their rivals and be the victorious 'last kite flying'. All of this was possible because kites could be easily made from readily available component parts such as silk, paper and bamboo, and because ancient people recognised the potential of such simple yet powerful devices.

Advancing a few centuries into European history to the Renaissance, we come across Leonardo da Vinci's 15th-century drawings of kites, which went on to inspire the technique used to create one of the first large suspension bridges at Niagara Falls 300 years later. His drawings of helicopters and his invention of the parachute, which gained little recognition at the time, are held in very high esteem by scientists and engineers today and we can see how elements of these designs still appear in modern kites.

In the 19th century, George Pocock, an English schoolteacher fascinated by kites and their potential, lifted his son 60m (200ft) on to a cliff top outside the city of Bristol to prove that it was possible to transport people using a kite. The boy then dismounted and slid safely back down the kite's line to earth as if on a zip-wire. In 1826 Pocock patented the 'Charvolant', a kite-propelled carriage which, although hard to steer, was very fast and had the additional benefit of inadvertently circumventing the toll charges levied at the time according to the number of horses pulling a carriage. Despite its impressive speed, however, the carriage was rumoured to offend the gentry when it overtook them and this, in addition to its haphazard handling, meant it never became a common mode of transport.

KITES ON SNOW

Fast-forward to the second half of the 20th century, when alpine-based kite flying was the first and most disciplined kite-related sport. Evolving from parachute-skiing and kite-skiing on frozen fields and lakes in the early 1970s, it has since gone on to become much more mainstream, despite the fact it can only be practised in very specific areas. Today, hosts of people in Britain and northern Europe don their kites and skis or snowboards at the slightest hint of the white stuff on the hills. As a result of the growth in media coverage of snowkiting events, the sport has also become more popular with mainstream water-based kiteboarders over the last decade, attracting

▶ **Snowkiting beginnings.**

world champions and big names to take part in snow-based adventures such as the 100km (62 miles) long Ragnarok endurance race in Hardangervidda, Norway. Here, alpine experience and snowkiting prowess come to the fore, with seasoned snowkiters and locals usually beating kiteboarding superstars to the podium, highlighting just how hard and technical it is to kite on the snow.

Experiencing the challenging vertiginous mountain environment has opened up a completely new world of possibilities for kiteboarders, iceboarders and kite buggyers alike, and has inspired the introduction of three-dimensional elements and specialist disciplines in the different environments. Sliders, kickers and all sorts of obstacles are now negotiated on the traditionally flat surfaces of locations such as Lake Silvaplana in Switzerland, adding another layer of excitement to the sports. Elsewhere, explorations on snow using kite power have propelled people such as *Top Gear*'s Richard Hammond as far as the North Pole. This separate progression of alpine kiting has been streamed into the 'youth and YouTube' melting-pot of

history, and a colourful, extreme evolution thrives in the European and American plateaus and mountains as well as in New Zealand, which boasts a small but expanding scene.

THE SPORT MOVES TO WATER

Jacob's Ladder was a famous UK-based project in the late 1970s that was spearheaded by four 'dare to be different' men with sailing and paragliding backgrounds from the south coast of Britain. These men, with a common vision of breaking a water speed record, embarked upon a five-year project to propel a small catamaran hull with flexifoil kites along a speed course.

From humble beginnings, this intrepid project saw a phenomenal increase in speed over four years – from 7 knots in its first speed week in 1978 (hosted by the Royal Yachting Association (RYA) in Weymouth and Portland), to a record-breaking 25 knots in 1982. Over the years, the project made use of three different hull designs, from a standard tornado catamaran hull to a custom-built hydrofoil. The kites were 'stacked' with flexifoil power kites, as was standard practice at this time,

▼ **Stacked foil kites.**

and delivered great power, limited control and a great many moments of surprise for the four men whose job of launching and recovering the kites kept the support boat extremely busy.

This project typifies the types of people you get in kite sports – those who have an idea and just run with it, against all the peer pressure, jeering, and the 'it'll never work' sceptics. Without substantial financial backing or medals to chase, the pioneering 'let's give it a go' attitude is a wonderful motivation, and something these four cannot help but smile about when retelling their story, which I was lucky enough to hear first-hand when I taught one of them to kiteboard in 2007.

In 1977, the Dutchman Gijsbertus Panhuise registered a patent whereby a pilot standing upright on a 'board' is pulled by a parachute tied to a harness. It seems, however, that this received little publicity and that no commercial backing followed. Less than a decade on, in Portland, Oregon, a cottage industry for 'kiteski' equipment was thriving. This was pioneered by Cory Roesler, who made kiteski wings in his shed after work with the help of his family. He then sold these to keen and brave waterskiers and windsurfers so that they could travel downwind along the coastline. Corey took his kiteski to Hawaii in the 1990s and, having gained a high level of expertise in its use, wowed the locals with his prowess and the equipment's capabilities. Having spent many years travelling around pioneering the kiteski, displaying its early potential at windsurfing and sailing events around the USA and beyond, Corey is rightly recognised as one of the pivotal innovators of modern kiteboarding.

Meanwhile, in the mid-1990s, the French Legaignoux brothers Bruno and Dominique were developing kiteboarding equipment that was eventually to bring the sport to the masses. Having designed and evolved their equipment through the mid-80s and 90s, these sailors, windsurfers and keen watersports enthusiasts were able to file a patent for the inflatable tube kite, along with designs for a 4-line bar, bow kite and bridled kite. Despite ten years' hard work, however, the inflatable tube kite never took off, perhaps due to the predominance of the windsurfing boom during this time and the brothers' limited resources and production capabilities. At this

▼ **Flying high.**

point they travelled to New Zealand, meeting designer and innovator Peter Lynn, then on to Hawaii, where they entered a licence agreement with windsurfing legends and equipment manufacturers Robby Naish and Don Montague.

At the same time, other breakthroughs in design and achievement were contributing to the rising popularity of this new extreme sport. In 1996, surfers extraordinaire Laird Hamilton and Emmanuel (Manu) Bertin gained mainstream TV coverage riding waves with kites, and 1997 saw the first specific kiteboard becoming available from French kite manufacturer, F-ONE, designed by Raphael Salles. In 1998, the first kiteboarding-specific international competition was held on Maui, which was won by Marcus 'Flash' Austin. Corey Roesler won the Johnnie Walker International Speed Sailing Trials in the sub-10m class. In 1999, Franz Olry designed the first production twin-tip, which again increased participation by making the board far easier to turn than directional boards had been.

All of this activity, and much more, in all corners of the world, ignited a flame of enthusiasm for the sport and progressed both human and equipment innovation around the world. The Legaignoux brothers created an equipment label in the late 1990s called Wipika, which was arguably the first kiteboarding brand. Once surfboard manufacturer Naish entered this market and created competition, the development of equipment increased dramatically.

The initial kite from Wipika was called the Classic, and had two lines and a control bar as well as a tiny hand pump for inflating the tubes. This enabled a boarder to consistently re-launch the kite from the water when it crashed, thus overcoming a significant problem that had been the cause of many long swims for early pioneers. Despite these innovations, kiteboarding remained very difficult, as I discovered for myself having managed

◀ **Robby Naish in action in 2004.**

to get one of these Wipika kites from Bruno himself around 1998. Together with a friend, I began attempting to use the kite with surfboards, windsurfing boards and wakeboards – in fact anything we could find – all with minimal success. This was a common trend and only the elite could travel to windward and maintain ground at this time, which in sailing is a fundamental skill.

KITEBOARDING GOES MAINSTREAM

Sometime in late 1999 the 4-line control bar became available, which for us changed everything. Within an hour we could go upwind, do a jump and even a rotation. This was helped by the fact that the first twin-tip boards were becoming widely available. These were symmetrical, like snowboards, and removed the need to gybe or tack, as you have to when windsurfing or sailing. Suddenly EVERYONE at the beach wanted a go. In the space of a year, some 100,000 people around the world took up the sport of kiteboarding. This in part was helped by the falling popularity of windsurfing in the later 90s as equipment became difficult to use and prohibitively elitist.

The year 2000 saw the explosion of the modern sport, and between late 2000 and 2005 manufacturers, participants, retailers, schools and holiday destinations all blossomed to meet the needs of the growing kiteboarding community. The next significant breakthrough occurred in 2006 when the 'bow kite' was produced by Cabrinha Kites (owned by Neil Pryde). The idea behind a bow kite was to increase the wind range and safety of the kite in order to reduce the number of accidents as well as the size of a boarder's 'quiver' – the number of kites required to cover all wind ranges. When asking students on instructor-training courses these days, it is not unusual to come up with a list of more than 100 specific kiteboarding-related manufacturers of hardware (kites and boards) and software (apparel, harnesses, wetsuits and related products), which shows how far the equipment has come since the early days. Better equipment enabled kiteboarders to travel further, faster, and in 2006 Kirsty Jones broke the long-distance world record by travelling 225km (149 miles) from Lanzarote in the Canary Islands to Morocco, Africa. Other long-distance journeys were made over the next few years, with Raphael Salles being part of the team who in 2007 navigated the 190km (120 miles) from St Tropez to Calvi. In 2008, Eric Gramond set a 420km (260-mile) distance record in 24 hours on Brazil's northeastern coastline.

Other areas of the sport also, quite literally, took off and 2009 was the year in which the first of two daredevil jumps by British Champion Lewis Crathern took place. The first of these was over Worthing Pier and, a year later, he also successfully jumped Brighton Pier. In 2010 the longest kiteboarding journey ever made was completed by Louis Tapper, along 2,000km (1,243 miles) of Brazil's trade wind-rich northeast coastline, and 2013 saw a team of six Dutch kiteboarders crossing the Atlantic Ocean from the Canary Islands to the Caribbean, taking shifts to maintain a continuous travel path. We can see from this that as the sport has continued to grow worldwide – breaking world records for: speed in 2017, when Alex Caizergues recorded over 57 knots; distance, where Francisco Lufinha travelled 862km (536 miles) in one non-stop journey from Lisbon to Maderia; in height, Maarten Haeger jumped an astonishing 34.8m into the air; and greatest numbers in a 'parade' was 596 kiters in 2019 at the the 'winds for future' kite event in Cumbuco, Brazil. The challenges are becoming ever greater and closer to the limits of human endurance and imagination: who knows what we will see in the future?

WHERE IT IS NOW

Over the first decade of the 21st century, various associations and governing bodies began to establish themselves in order to regulate standards in competition, training and participation internationally. The International Kiteboarding Association (IKA) is now the recognised class regulator of the sport, and is a sub-committee of World Sailing (WS). Their broad role is to formalise and globally administrate competitions and participation in the sport. They were instrumental in lobbying to bring kiteboarding into the 2016 Olympics as a recognised discipline (although this decision was later overturned), but a successful inclusion is guaranteed for the Paris 2024 games for both men and women in kite hydrofoil racing.

Competition has evolved and changed dramatically over the last decade, as have the styles and disciplines in which a kiteboarder can compete. Currently there are three defined disciplines within kiteboarding: racing, waveriding and freestyle. These generic categories can then be further broken down. For example, freestyle incorporates big air, which is gaining popularity in recent years with events like the Red Bull King of the Air, in Cape Town, attracting huge crowds. Racing has become professional, with an Olympics looming, and the regulation foiling equipment enables speeds of almost four times the wind speed on the course and a minimum of 5 knots on the course, allowing racing in almost any conditions. Waveriding and foiling freestyle disciplines are also adding into the expression categories of the sport and progressing in technicality at an impressive speed. I will explain the competition structure both nationally and internationally in more depth in the relevant section later in the book.

LOOKING FORWARD

As you read this book, people are kiteboarding all over the world – from the frigid waters of Iceland and Alaska to the crystal blue tropics of the Caribbean. Television channels and social media websites dedicated to the sport thrive online, while countless companies produce equipment and products for the expanding kiteboarding market, estimated these days to be worth some US $250 million annually, with over 1.5 million people actively participating. Considering its short history, these figures demonstrate the incredible growth of the sport and it gives me pleasure to remember that I was able to enjoy (most of the time...) being there early on, and played a small part in kiteboarding's growth into an established and extreme sport of the 21st century. Long may it continue!

► **Alex Caizergues competes in Perth.**

02

Air

Air

The basic element we need in order to fly a kite is wind. Once we have this fundamental source of power we can generate some other vital components that will work with this energy. Let's start at the beginning and build the elements up one by one to gain a full understanding.

HOW DOES A KITE FLY?

DRAG

Provided there is some airflow/wind we can get things to fly. The most simplistic form of kite is a diamond shape made from a framework of two crossed sticks with some material stretched over it. When placed in a current of air, this shape generates drag if it is restricted by a line, which we can also hold and use to control the kite. Wind hits the windward surface of the kite, which is prevented from blowing away by the flying line. The opposing forces create tension on the line, which is 'drag'. The larger the kite the greater the dragging force created.

These kites are frequently people's first experience of a kite and, as generations of children can testify, they are both simple to use and safe. The streamer often attached to the bottom corner is there to create stability and extra drag, which keeps the kite facing up, as well as looking good. The main restriction with these kites is that there is no real steering potential and they are extremely inefficient, so their use is restricted to play.

LIFT

Once drag has been achieved, lift can be generated by refining the shape of the kite: the more efficient the shape, the greater the lift. Perhaps the best example of an ideal shape for creating lift is an aeroplane's wing profile. Lift is generated because air flows over the upper and lower surfaces of a wing at slightly different speeds. The airflow on the upper surface has further to travel and therefore 'spreads out' as it travels faster, creating a lower pressure relative to that of the airflow over the lower surface of the wing. Hence 'lift' is generated upwards, from the area of greater pressure to the one of lower pressure.

This lift can be maximised in a number of ways: by speeding up the airflow rate (which basically is wind speed); increasing the surface area of the object; accelerating the object's own speed through the air (which can often generate much more lifting force than that which can be created by the existing wind speed); and finally by modifying the object's shape. We only have to look at the differing designs for aeroplane wings to realise that although the basics are generic, there is no optimum shape yet.

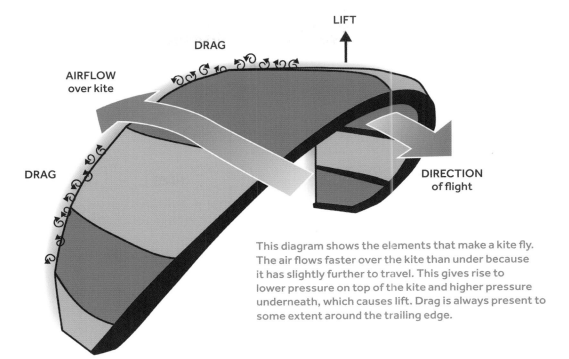

LIFT

DRAG

AIRFLOW
over kite

DRAG

DIRECTION
of flight

This diagram shows the elements that make a kite fly.
The air flows faster over the kite than under because
it has slightly further to travel. This gives rise to
lower pressure on top of the kite and higher pressure
underneath, which causes lift. Drag is always present to
some extent around the trailing edge.

The design of a modern-day kite is based on analogous
principles and works in a similar way, although the ability
to easily relaunch aeroplane wings is not top of the design
specifications at Airbus, unlike at Naish and other kite
manufacturers. Countless variations on this principle are
invented, adopted, evolved and cast aside as we learn
more about aerodynamics. However, whereas most wings,
spoilers and air-efficient items deal with wind coming
mainly from the front – as can be seen in racing cars
and bikes, aeroplanes and even most types of vessel –
kiteboarding has taken the 'engine' (the kite) and allowed
it to be thrown across the sky from side to side, rotated
through 360 degrees and more, and even being momentarily
positioned below its own anchoring axis. These factors have
sparked some interesting theories and push the laws of
aerodynamics in new and exciting directions.

ANGLE OF ATTACK

Once a kite has airflow going over it, creating both drag
and lift, it will fly in the wind window (see page 28) and
naturally sit at the zenith or 12 o'clock secure position
in the right amount of laminar wind (streamlined wind

flowing in parallel layers) for its size. In order to position
the kite correctly to achieve this, the pilot can alter the
angle of attack, which refers to the angle of the kite's
canopy in relation to the wind flowing over it. This has a big
effect on the performance of the wing. A kiteboarder does
this by using a control bar to fly their kite. The trimming
system on the bar allows the pilot to push the bar away,
decreasing the kite's angle of attack and depowering it, or
pulling it in, which increases both the angle of attack and
the level of power. Get it wrong, however, and the kite may
crash, stall or even fly backwards.

The major breakthrough for kiteboarding came about,
as we have already discovered, in 1999, when the 4-line
control bar system was first introduced to leading edge
inflatable (LEI) or tube kites. This allowed the pilot to
very easily alter the angle of attack with much more
precision, just as the pilot of an aircraft can modify the
surface of wings. Anyone who has watched the wings
of a landing plane after touchdown will tell you they
change shape quite dramatically; from a smooth wing
profile for flying they segment at the back after landing,

with some sections pointing down at an angle of 45 degrees and others pointing up at the same angle. This breaks up the smooth profile and helps to slow the plane down by creating extra drag once it is on the ground. A kiteboarder can create a similar effect on their kite by trimming the bar in or out. On LEI kites specifically, pulling the bar towards the pilot increases the angle of attack and therefore generates more lift and consequent power, provided the trim angle is set correctly and the kite is moving first. By releasing the bar, the angle of attack is reduced, along with subsequent power and lift.

This advancement suddenly meant a pilot could 'sheet out' during a 'gust' (increased moment of wind speed) and spill excess power rather than incurring the inevitable wipeout that would previously have occurred. All sailing craft have the same capability through their mainsail halyard, which allows them to increase and decrease the sail's angle to the wind. Kites however,

being supported entirely by the wind, must get this angle right at all times or risk the kite crashing to the ground. The angle of attack at its optimum produces the most speed, lift and power from the kite.

Reducing the angle of attack correspondingly reduces the speed, power and lift it can generate.

Increasing the angle of attack beyond a certain point – which is different for all kites and wind strengths – creates inefficiency over the canopy that can negate the power, lift and speed, and the flow of air can also reverse, creating a 'stalling' effect. For LEI kites, this is a negative effect and results in loss of momentum and control.

A skilled pilot can generate the greatest possible amount of speed and efficiency from a kite and use these to jump, head to windward or simply go fast without stalling the kite. This is a fine balance and a good skill to gain.

▼ **Angle of attack.**

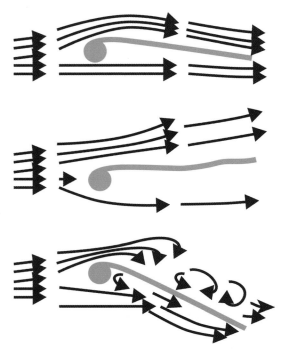

Correct angle, producing maximum speed, lift and power.

Decreased angle, which reduces canopy tension along the trailing edge, resulting in decreased speed, power and lift.

Increased angle, which can create a 'stalling effect'.

▲ **Steering is logical and intuitive; the harder you pull, the faster the kite will turn.**

STEERING

In order to generate power in the right direction the kite must be flown through the correct zone of the wind window at the right time. Steering is very straightforward and logical. If you wish the kite to turn right, pull on the right side of the bar and vice versa to turn left. The harder the bar is pulled the faster the kite reacts and the more aggressively it turns. In practice this is easy both to comprehend and to execute with a range of kites. It is, however, useful to understand exactly what happens in technical terms, especially for those wanting their kite to perform better, for instance in competitions or to go faster or higher.

Steering results from a localised alteration of the angle of attack. The motion of pulling on a sideline at the control bar results in an increased angle of attack over the tensioned wing tip. This increased angle creates more drag and slows down this side of the kite.

The opposite wing tip has not been subjected to the same angle change; in fact the angle of attack on the opposing side can be slightly reduced. This allows the opposing side to continue at the same speed or even slightly increase in speed, so turning the kite.

Whatever the conditions, there is inevitably a time lapse between moving the bar and the kite turning. This delay can be very small with strong winds, small kites and positive pilot inputs to the bar. However, the lighter the winds, the larger the kite and the more diluted the inputs, the slower the reaction time of the kite and the corresponding output power and turning speed.

'Adverse yaw' is a further factor that is apparent when a kite turns. This phenomenon can be explained as a momentary shift of load towards the non-tensioned side of the kite before the real loading effect occurs on the tensioned line. The levels of tension commonly applied to steer a kite override and negate this effect, although it can sometimes be visually observed on larger kites in light winds.

When turning, a kite can do so 'reactively' or 'progressively'. These terms describe the way in which the kite turns around its own axis. A reactively turning kite can turn quickly, pivoting around one wing tip, which allows fast redirection of the kite without gaining excess power. This can be useful in some dynamic waveriding and freestyle manoeuvres. Progressive turning is when the kite continues forwards as it is turning, regardless of the tightness of the turning angle – imagine a train on a track that can only turn at a certain angle while remaining on the tracks. Kites that do this are generally larger and better suited to racing and speed-related disciplines, although freestyle big air kiteloopers can benefit from this type of turning if they are up to the challenge.

WHERE A KITE FLIES

THE 'STATIC' WIND WINDOW

During this section I will refer to the person flying the kite as the 'pilot'. All kites fly within a wind window. This is the generic name given to the area downwind of the pilot that the kite lines will allow the kite to fly in. The longer the lines, the larger this wind window is from side to side.

The shape of the wind window can be described as a quarter of a sphere positioned downwind of the pilot. Even when stationary, the wind window can pivot around a pilot with wind shifts and gusts, when the wind suddenly and sharply increases in strength. The wind window can't be seen visually, but will always exist downwind of the pilot, whose location determines the central pivoting point of the window.

▼ **The static wind window. This illustration shows three different views of the same window. Diagram A is bird's eye view, B is the rear view and C is the side view.**

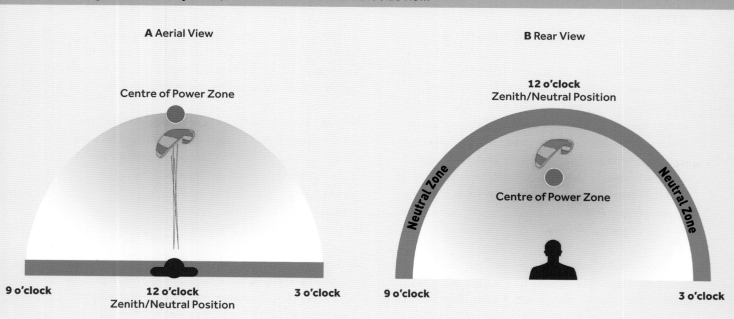

A Aerial View

Centre of Power Zone

9 o'clock

12 o'clock
Zenith/Neutral Position

3 o'clock

B Rear View

12 o'clock
Zenith/Neutral Position

Neutral Zone

Neutral Zone

Centre of Power Zone

9 o'clock

3 o'clock

There are three zones within the wind window:

1 **The neutral/static zone** This area represents the edge of the flying window. In good wind, the kite can rest and be stationary, producing little or no power in this zone. I will often refer to positions within the neutral zone as times on a traditional clock face. You can see below in Diagram B of the static wind window that the kite can be held stable at all times between 9 o'clock, (the left-hand-side launch spot) through 12 o'clock (above the pilot's head) to 3 o'clock (the right-hand-side launch spot).

2 **The intermediate/soft zone** This is the area just downwind of the neutral zone, in which the kite starts to move dynamically and produces power. The power generated in the intermediate zone is gradual and increases progressively towards the centre-point of the window where the power zone resides.

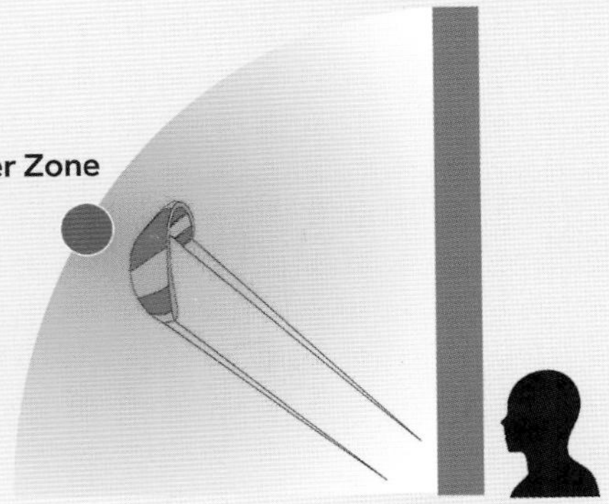

The easiest way to get used to this zone is by flying a small training kite above your head between 11 and 1 o'clock in a figure-of-eight pattern of movement. As you become more used to this and gain confidence you can increase the speed and positivity through the bar and enlarge the size of the figure-of-eight. This increased movement and speed will augment the line tension and power. A key point when steering the kite is to use the bar like a set of bicycle handlebars, pushing and pulling, keeping the bar horizontal.

3 **The power zone** This is the exciting bit, but it is also the area that can be dangerous if not used with sensible control. The centre of the power zone is around halfway up in the wind window, directly downwind from the pilot as seen in Diagram C of the static wind window. This area gives the best mix of upwards lift and sideways drag and exposes the greatest area of the kite's surface to the wind.

The power zone is a purely dynamic zone and the kite cannot be paused or stopped while in it – it will continue to fly towards the neutral zone/edge of the window.

Most kites are given lines of 20–25m (66–82ft) in length, which means the kite can be flown high, free from ground turbulence, yet retain a good reaction speed, which is lost as line length increases.

C Side View

12 o'clock
Zenith/Neutral Position

Centre of Power Zone

9 o'clock

GRADIENT WIND

Gradient wind is a factor affecting a kite within the wind window. In simple terms it is the increase of wind speed that occurs as you rise in height from the Earth's high-friction surface (check the wind speed next time you are flying in an aeroplane). For kiteboarders, it means that closer to the ground there is both less wind and more turbulence because of ground friction, while higher in the sky there is more wind and less turbulence.

THE 'DYNAMIC' WIND WINDOW

Once you begin to move, the static window changes dramatically and becomes dynamic. It is still governed by the location of the pilot, who remains the pivoting and origin point of the window, but when this origin point is moving an extra force known as 'apparent wind' is introduced. The angle at which the kite can fly and the pilot can travel is now controlled by a combination of factors:

TRUE WIND This is the direction of airflow across the ground.

INDUCED WIND This is the wind created once a pilot begins to move. Induced wind could also be described as 'direction of travel' of the pilot, which has the same effect.

APPARENT WIND This is the combination of the true wind blowing and the speed and angle that the pilot travels across the surface (or air, but that is a whole different story). This is explained in greater depth on pages 116–17.

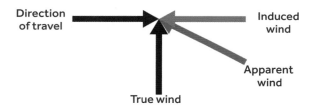

Equipment advances such as larger fins and very efficient kite designs have made kiteboarding the fastest wind sport discipline to windward, achieving incredible angles and speeds. For kiteboard racers the relationship between speed over the ground and the angle achievable to windward is the difference between first and last place.

The key to successful kiteboarding at every level is a good solid understanding and familiarity with the wind window and how this affects the kite and thus the pilot's potential to use a range of kites, from basic foils upwards. A strong knowledge-base will help every aspect, from learning the basics to progressing and eventually competing. Take a look at a professional freestyle kiteboarder mid-handle-pass and they certainly won't be looking at the kite; they know, from experience and practice, exactly what it is doing and how best to utilise the wind window. In addition to slowing down your progress both on the water and along the learning curve, a lack of basic kite-flying skills can result in many kite crashes, so it is well worth practising!

WHERE WIND COMES FROM

Weather, in the most simplistic terms, is caused by heat. Hot air rises from warmer regions of the planet, travels and then cools as it reaches cooler areas. This is due to defined currents and airstreams around the globe. Some of these are large, consistently flowing rivers of air, and others are tiny localised weather systems in a specific area at a certain time of year.

▼ The dynamic wind window is the segment of the window that the kite flies in when moving. This is best imagined as a cheese wedge across and in front of the pilot.

To start with the basics, the warmest region of the planet is around the equator and approximately 30 degrees north and south of it. The coldest regions are from 40 degrees towards the poles.

LOW-PRESSURE SYSTEMS

Once a region of low pressure has been formulated through rising heat and a surrounding area of higher pressure, this weather system – which can span 500m (1,640ft) in width and move at over 112kph (70mph) – moves on the higher atmosphere winds and collects moisture, and often strength, over water. Over land these low-pressure systems generally lose their moisture as rain and decrease in intensity as their flow and energy is disrupted and, therefore, dissipated by the ground beneath.

The big boys of the low-pressure world are the North Atlantic depressions originating in the Gulf of Mexico and the eastern seaboard of the USA, which are then bowled across the North Atlantic towards Europe's west coast – much to the excitement of kiteboarders, surfers and windsurfers alike. These can unleash some ferocious conditions on the western coasts of Ireland, England, France, Spain and Portugal, putting these places on the map as hardcore big-wave and strong-wind winter draws for the hardy watermen of the world. Low-pressure systems in the northern hemisphere rotate in an anticlockwise direction, while in the southern hemisphere they move clockwise. In both hemispheres a pressure of below 1,013 millibars is classed as low pressure, with pressures below 980 millibars resulting in strong storms and those below 950 millibars often causing severe flooding, damage and swells.

Carrying vast amounts of moisture as clouds, these depressions will have a warm front leading its track across the skies, containing low clouds, drizzle and a 'close' atmosphere. The cold front follows at a greater speed and will contain the lion of the cloud world, the cumulonimbus, which can produce severe squalls, winds shifts and increases in speed. These present dangers to kiteboarders and should be avoided.

HIGH-PRESSURE SYSTEMS

The opposite of a low-pressure system or depression is an area of high pressure. As its name suggests, this area is higher in pressure and results in descending air flowing clockwise in the northern hemisphere. The descending air prevents clouds forming through rising moisture and generally results in stable weather, clear skies and lighter winds. Temperatures often drop, especially at night, during 'ridges' of high pressure, which can sit and linger for several weeks at a time.

CLOUDS

When air is cooled to such an extent that it becomes saturated clouds form. The cooling process primarily occurs as warmer air rises and subsequently cools. The tiny water droplets that are formed during this process create clouds. At temperatures below about -20°C (-4°F) these droplets can freeze, creating ice crystals, which can fall as sleet or snow depending on their adiabatic cooling speed. Adiabatic cooling can be measured by the 'lapse rate' of warm air, heated at and by the Earth's surface rising. This warm, less dense air rises and cools, losing its energy. At a certain point, during this cooling ascension, the air mass will cross its dew point. It's at this point that the air condenses causing clouds, which eventually lead to precipitation.

Classified by Luke Howard in the early 1800s, there are Latin terms to describe different types of condensing air masses at varying altitudes:

- Cirrus (tuft or filament)
- Cumulus (heap or pile)
- Stratus (a layer)
- Nimbus (rain-bearing)

There are around ten common cloud types, which are all referred to using a combination of these generic terms. 'Alto' is added to the terms to signify high and medium-level formations.

High clouds are commonly composed of ice crystals and have a base 5,500–14,000m (18,000–45,000ft) above ground level. These clouds are less dense and more settled than other types, which is why aeroplanes cruise in the middle of this zone at 10,500m (35,000ft), a region that is commonly stable and efficient in terms of air density. There are three main types of high cloud:

- Cirrus – white filaments.
- Cirrocumulus – small rippled elements.
- Cirrostratus – transparent sheet, often with white haloes.

Medium-level clouds are found between 2,000–5,500m (6,500–18,000ft) and are composed of both frozen and non-frozen water droplets. These are described as:

- Altocumulus – layered, rippled elements, generally with white and light grey.
- Altostratus – thin layer, light to medium grey letting the sun shine through a haze or frozen-glass effect.

- Nimbostratus – thicker layer that can block the sun at a lower level, darker at the base. These can contain rain or snow, sometimes falling very heavily.

Low clouds are typically dense, dark, contain non-frozen water droplets and exist below 2,000m (6,500ft).

- Stratocumulus – white, rolled and fluffy with grey shading.
- Stratus – grey with a layered level base.
- Cumulus – independent, vertical towers of rolling mounds with a flat defined base.
- Cumulonimbus – a heaping, towering rain-bearing cloud, bringing heavy rain and wind anomalies. Can be likened to cauliflowers.

STORMS, HURRICANES AND CYCLONES

While none of these weather events are ideal for beginner or intermediate kiteboarders, in recent years, along with the birth of global storm-chasing competitions like the Billabong XXL and Red Bull Storm Chaser, these

▼ **Cross section of a cold front.**

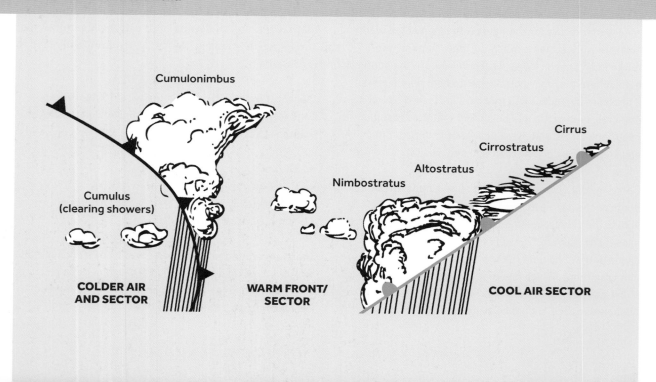

conditions have become popular; experts and crazy men and women study weather charts and fly around the globe in search of the biggest and gnarliest storms to conquer. Many of these events are prevalent in the North Atlantic wintertime, when they batter the western shores of Europe and North Africa between September and February when water temperatures reach a chilly 6ºC (43ºF). They are referred to as hurricanes when they are above a force 10 on the Beaufort Wind Scale.

Tropical storms occur above waters with a temperature of over 26ºC (79ºF) for longer periods. This heat can create storms of great intensity and they are most common above both of the tropics in summertime, when the sun evaporates huge quantities of water into clouds that can very quickly form deep areas of low pressure and winds exceeding 217kph (135mph). The South Atlantic escapes these violent storms because it has a lower ambient water temperature. While Atlantic and eastern Pacific storms are referred to as 'hurricanes', tropical storms are termed as 'cyclones' in the Indian Ocean and 'typhoons' in the Asian Pacific.

Most regions of the world are typically subject to two seasons, one hot and one cooler or wetter, while spring and autumn signify the change between the two states. These seasons occur during opposite months of the year in the northern and southern hemispheres. The equatorial regions are the exception, where temperatures maintain a pleasant 25–30ºC (77–86ºF) year round. This is because the Earth's annual orbit around the sun tilts to around 23.5 degrees then back again between the tropics of Cancer and Capricorn, which means that temperatures remain fairly constant.

SEA AND LAND BREEZES

Water and air cool at different speeds, which allows landmasses to dramatically heat during the course of a sunny day, while the seas and oceans warm at far slower seasonal rates. During the hot part of the day, heat rises from this warm land and creates a localised 'low' pressure area. Cooler air rushes in from the sea to fill the gap and try to even out the pressure. For us

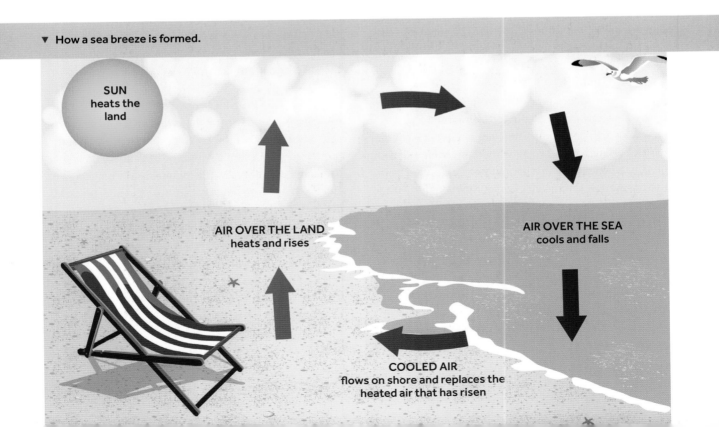

▼ **How a sea breeze is formed.**

SUN heats the land

AIR OVER THE LAND heats and rises

AIR OVER THE SEA cools and falls

COOLED AIR flows on shore and replaces the heated air that has risen kiteboarders this creates a great afternoon onshore breeze, which in certain regions is as regular as the tide.

Much of the inner-Mediterranean's watersports industry is built on this effect, which can extend as little as 500m (1,630ft) out to sea from the coastline. It can either enhance an existing wind direction or simply create a breeze where previously utter calm prevailed. The strength rarely exceeds a moderate breeze and is strongest in mid- to late afternoon. Its creation can also signify its demise in certain areas if the rising warm air is rich in moisture, which will condense, forming clouds that then block the sun's warming rays and stop the landmass heating further.

During the night, the opposite of a sea breeze can be found. As quickly as land gains heat it can lose it, and its temperature can fall below the residual temperature of the surrounding sea. This can result in a light offshore breeze as the sun sets and rises. For this reason it is never a great idea to sail during these times as this effect is somewhat of a disaster for a kiteboarder as the wind drops from 18 knots to 5 knots and swings offshore!

TRADE WINDS

Popular with sailors and kiteboarders alike, these winds blow towards the equator from around 30 degrees north and south. They are deflected west due to the Coriolis effect, which is the deflection of moving objects when placed in a rotating object (in this case the Earth) that rotates clockwise. Northeasterly trade winds in the northern hemisphere and southeasterly trade winds in the southern hemisphere are most consistent through the warmer months of summer. This area is referred to as the Hadley cell and creates a huge sea-breeze effect. The warm air rises away from the equator with high moisture content over oceanic regions, then travels north and south at altitude before descending to the surface again at around 30 degrees.

Known as the 'trades' these reliable, warm and moderate breezes became the favoured routes used from the 14th century by sailors and the shipping trade, propelling them in good time across the world's oceans, establishing consistent trading patterns for goods, slaves and the discovery of new worlds, extending up to 30 degrees north and south of the equator.

By contrast, the rising hot air along the 'equatorial low' creates no surface or horizontal airflow and has been nicknamed the 'doldrums': this is not the place for your next kiteboarding holiday. Neither is the region in both hemispheres between where the trades and the 'roaring forties' originate, around 30–40 degrees. Sailors through history were becalmed in these zones for such long periods they had to take to eating their horses to survive.

The 'roaring forties', 'furious fifties' and 'shrieking sixties' become progressively windier towards the poles as airflow gains momentum in a generally westerly direction north and south. The relatively stable polar highs feed cold air into these westerly zones producing a Ferrel cell in both hemispheres. This huge-scale mixing of subtropical warm air and polar cold air is the primary cause of the diverse, unstable and eclectic weather that Europe experiences.

ATLANTIC OCEAN

Northern Atlantic wintertime is known for its stormy seas, cold water, wetter weather and shorter days. It has the highest average wind speed of above 35 knots combined with some of the roughest seas and coldest storms. It can frequently range from the mid-teens in degrees Celsius to the same in minus values within 24 hours and is greatly affected by the wind direction. For example, a southwesterly wind could bring 10ºC (50ºF) and rain in January to the UK, followed by -1–5ºC (30–23ºF) with clear skies a day later if the wind veered to the north. The jet stream provides a consistent east to west track for weather originating on the eastern seaboard of the USA, and weather fronts travel on this generally southwesterly airstream towards northern

Europe, providing a relatively warming and moisture-plentiful lifeline to this region.

PACIFIC OCEAN

This is the largest ocean by far, covering almost 30 per cent of the world's surface. At its deepest point, in terms of volume it could contain almost all the landmass of the planet. The Pacific is a vast and diverse place and it can generate massive storms in the northern hemisphere's 30-60 degrees of latitude zones in January, producing many of the huge waves that are responsible for immortalising Hawaiian watermen. With greater ocean depths rising suddenly on to mid-ocean islands it produces the world's biggest consistent swells with more moderate winter temperatures and often lower wind speeds.

Very consistent trade winds through the summer give great winds in the mid-ocean islands, from China to Chile. The subtropical southern hemisphere island chains receive sun, world-class surf and lighter winds, and are some of the world's most popular tourist paradises. Polynesia and Fiji are two examples of key destinations, but there are many others.

Southeast Asia's strong northwesterly monsoon dominates the western Pacific in January and reverses during July, giving two distinct seasons that are capitalised upon by kitesports. The South China Sea produces strong January winds and storms while the west-wind zone blows strong between New Zealand and South America. The southern hemisphere's summer

▼ **Global wind patterns and trade winds.**

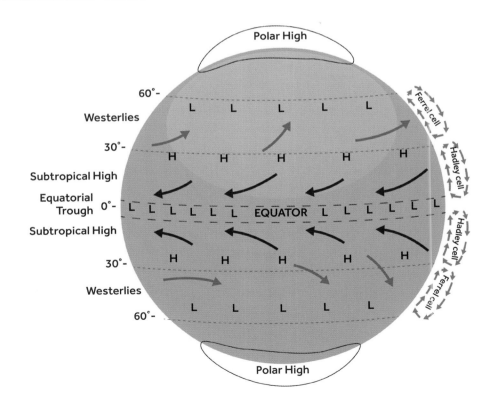

feeds off a stable high in the far South Pacific, producing strong and powerful southerly winds and swells along the west coast of South America.

INDIAN OCEAN

The Indian Ocean is generally a warm ocean and sees the strongest far-south-formulated storms, sending fierce warm winds and swell towards Mauritius and Indo/Micronesia. The Southern Indian Ocean, although rarely frequented for kiteboarding, is considered the nemesis for sailing's elite circumnavigation races. Defined trade winds through the Gulf of Bengal and around Africa's horn, and Western Australia's infamous sea breeze winds are all enhanced by huge landmasses, which feed these effects and strengthen their force.

AIRFLOW AND LOCAL WIND PHENOMENA

LAMINAR FLOW

This type of flow is a continuous, steady and constant flow of all the air particles at the same speed in the same direction. Imagine a deep and slowly flowing river – there is no real disturbance in the water and if you drop a leaf in it will float along on the current. Air can do the same as the water, although its flow

can reach higher speeds than those of liquids. Under mechanical pressure – such as a hosepipe – however, both liquids and gases can achieve great laminar pressures.

Laminar flow is what kiteboarders are looking for, as it is an orderly and smooth current that we can then use to create motion, lift and drag in a controlled sense. Kiteboarders rarely use the term laminar, but a smile at the end of a session often means the wind was 'good' and laminar in flow.

LAMINAR FLOW

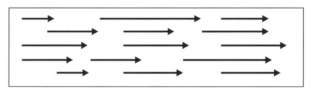

TURBULENT FLOW

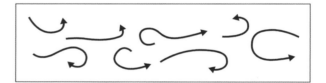

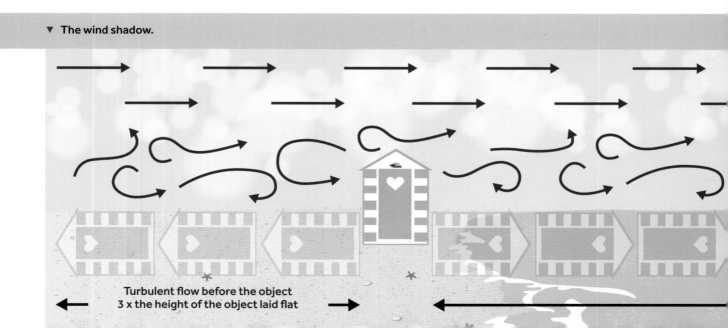

▼ The wind shadow.

Turbulent flow before the object
3 x the height of the object laid flat

TURBULENT FLOW

Just as kiteboarders rarely use the word 'laminar', they also rarely describe wind as 'turbulent'; a more common term would be 'gusty', referring to non-constant speed of the wind. No kiteboarder I have met to date dreams of gusty winds, because turbulent flow has no pattern or trend – it is completely random in its motion and therefore allows no stability or control for a kite flying through this type of air. While laminar flow exists in areas where there are no obstacles, turbulent flow is created by the presence of objects, and the density, size and shape of these objects determines the extent of the turbulence. Imagine water flowing down a shallow rocky stream; the air above the land often resembles this, which is why offshore winds tend to be bad for kiteboarding as they are gusty from having crossed a bumpy landscape (and will blow you away from land).

There are infinite causes of turbulent flow, from a single tree on a desert island to a city of tower blocks, but whatever the cause it is best avoided when kiteboarding. There are a number of different marked effects that can occur to airflow and kiteboarders in these areas:

COMPRESSION Compression is a common and potentially dangerous wind effect, which occurs along the shoreline in onshore winds. A steep rise in the land from sea level compresses the low-level wind upwards into the flow above. This squashing effect increases the speed of the wind over the top of an obstacle, which is why we always feel more wind when we are standing on a hill above a beach. This effect can result in the doubling of the normal wind speed. There is no real way a kiteboarder can use compression wind to their advantage safely. So remember don't fly your kite above raised land or obstacles on the beach.

CONVERGENCE/VENTURI EFFECT The Venturi effect can be the difference between there being enough wind to go kiteboarding and not on a given day, if you know where to look and understand how it works. It is a positive effect, whereby the wind speed is increased between two landmasses or large objects by compressing it and forcing it to move quicker through the restricted space. It is often found in estuaries and 'straits' where there is water between two relatively close landmasses. The same effect can be felt in cities between buildings, although this form is of no real use to kiteboarders.

WIND SHADOW AND TURBULENT FLOW As wind flows around and over objects it does many dynamic but unpredictable things, including becoming turbulent, reversing in direction, and increasing or decreasing in strength.

Behind (to leeward or downwind of) an object it is common to experience an area where the flow is reduced to almost nothing – just like the downstream side of a rock in a stream or river. This effect is often seen with offshore winds, where it feels like there is no wind on the beach yet out to sea the wind is strong.

A general rule of thumb is that an area seven times the height of an object downwind will be negatively affected. It can also be negatively affected by an order of three times upwind of a large object. The shape and size of the object dictates the magnitude of this effect.

Turbulent flow after the object
7 x the height of the object laid flat

THE BAY EFFECT Within larger curved-shaped bays you often find kiteboarders and wind enthusiasts at the downwind end. This is no coincidence, as there will be a combination of convergence and friction at this spot where the airflow meets the land's surface. This results in a slight increase in wind strength and a more onshore angle to the wind, making it both safer and stronger – and explaining why this often then becomes the most-frequented location on a larger beach.

An almost opposite effect caused when wind and the coastline interact is the wind hugging the coast. As the airflow is compressed and turned along a mountainous coastline it can increase the wind by a force or two. This is the case along the west coast of South America along the Andes mountain range.

KATABATIC Also known as 'fall winds', these occur where colder high-density air descends downwards on a hill or mountainside. They can result in some strong wind

speeds and give rise to some very popular kiteboarding destinations. The main areas where these winds are found are the Arctic mountains and plains as well as around large capes or headlands. The ones we often experience as kiteboarders are warm in temperature by the time they meet sea level and can create consistently good conditions for kiteboarding.

ANABATIC These are known as 'up-slope winds' and gain their name from the ancient Greek verb 'anabainein' meaning 'to rise'. They are most commonly found in mountainous regions and occur in calm weather through convection heating. For instance, if a mountain top has the sun beating down on it, the air around it will be warmed and consequently will rise. The cooler air beneath, which may have been shadowed by the mountain, rises in an attempt to equalise the locally created low pressure and warms in temperature as it does so. It is not uncommon, however, for this rising air to cool adiabatically (meaning it condenses as it rises

▼ **The bay effect.**

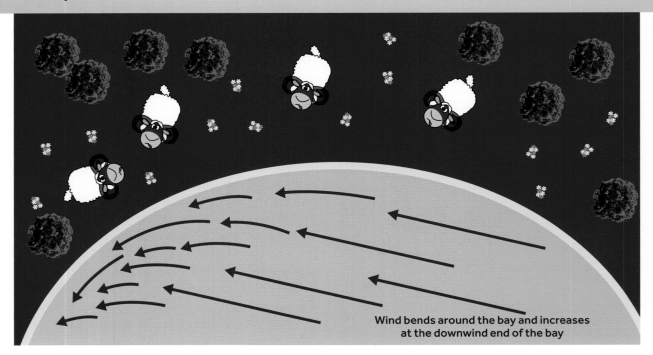

Wind bends around the bay and increases at the downwind end of the bay

and cools) to its dew point and for clouds to form, which can deliver rain or even thunder, and slow or stop the anabatic process by blocking the sun's direct rays.

This effect is rarely experienced by kiteboarders on the water but is a sought-after effect for snowkiters and paragliders alike in mountainous regions.

ALTITUDE WINDS As you climb in altitude a few things happen to air: generally it cools, thins in density and can therefore flow at far greater rates. The airflow at 10,500m (35,000ft), which is standard cruising height for a commercial airline, is often in excess of 322kph (200mph). These winds generally don't affect kiteboarders, but can be used by snowkiters and others up on the slopes of a mountain.

WIND DENSITY It is not uncommon for kiteboarders in South Africa or parts of the Caribbean to learn in and enjoy winds well above 30 knots in speed. Yet attempting to use the same wind speeds in colder regions such as northern Europe is extreme and often dangerous. This is because wind is not only affected by altitude – it gets thinner and faster with height – but it also gets denser, even viscous, when it is cold. So while a kiteboarder cruising the fjords of Iceland in February is quite happy on a 9m (30ft) board in 15 knots, a kiteboarder in the same wind strength on Brazil's famous northeast coastline would need over 20 knots to feel the same power and comfort.

The density of dry air can be calculated using the Ideal Gas Law, but I have never met a kiteboarder applying this to their choice of kite size around the globe. Experience and a small level of understanding should suffice, and alert you to the need for exercising caution and using a small, appropriate kite when kiteboarding in cold and stormy conditions.

FORECASTING

Kiteboarding was lucky enough to grow up in an age of accurate weather forecasting both locally and worldwide. Trends are commonly known about around the globe, as are local effects in a specific spot; no kiteboarders flock to Cape Town or western Australia in July when humid, windless days are the norm, and likewise there is no dawn patrol culture in the Greek summertime, when afternoon winds arrive after lunch.

The Internet is undoubtedly the greatest source of information, predicting the weather, wind, temperature and swell in one information-rich, easy-to-read forecast. Other media such as TV, radio and newspapers as well as local knowledge can also be used to plan your next session. The key here is to take forecasts with a pinch of salt and not assume they are always right – using a combination of several forecasts is usually the best plan. Also, make an effort to learn and remember seasonal trends and local effects for your own spot, along with potential dangers that can occur.

Visual forecasting is an art that can very effectively be done through studying the clouds and sky. Paragliders pay extra-special attention to these visual clues over and above any forecast on a given day of flying. They can be the difference between a great clear sky session and disaster.

Some useful websites to check are:
www.windguru.cz
www.magicseaweed.com

www.seabreeze.com.au
www.surfline.com
www.xcweather.co.uk

Water

03

Water

The water underneath you when kiteboarding is often just as changeable as the air above, and for that reason it is equally as important to know what it is doing and what effect it will have on the conditions (and therefore you). A location can go from a flat, waist-deep lagoon with no current to a dry sharp reef or a rough, fast-moving current with large waves in a matter of an hour or two. Fortunately, tides are completely reliable and their highs and lows can be predicted for years into the future.

TIDES AND CURRENTS

Tides affect the water in two ways: vertically, which can be measured by their range in distance between high tide and low tide; and horizontally, whereby their flow or stream is measured in knots, and changes in direction and speed through the tidal cycle. A greater tidal range results in a greater speed of horizontal flow.

The range of the tide can differ greatly from one location to another but the time between a high tide and low tide is generally six hours the world over. Typically the time of high tide moves on around 45 minutes each day, which gives a complete cycle of the tide in 28 days. This includes two 'spring' and two 'neap' tidal cycles.

FORMULATION

Tides are caused by the sun and the gravitational pull of the moon on the water in our oceans as it elliptically orbits the Earth, taking 28 days to do so. The moon is far closer to us than the sun, which is why it has a greater gravitational effect. The moon's gravitational pull creates a water mound or bulge towards it on the Earth's surface, while centrifugal force dictates a similar bulge on the opposite site of the globe. The wave length between these mounds is 21,000km (13,000 miles) which, when combined with the Earth's 24-hour rotational cycle, provides two high tides and two low tides daily. This can be referred to as a 'semi-diurnal' tide and is the most common type.

Although accurate and predictable, tides can be greatly affected by atmospheric pressure, sea states and winds. The combination of a high spring tide, onshore wind and large sea state can result in coastal flooding and extremely high water levels. These occur rarely in synchronicity but can have incredible effects if all three forces coincide.

SPRING AND NEAP TIDES

During the moon's orbit it aligns with the sun and Earth twice, on the new and full moons, which are approximately 14 days apart. When this happens the tidal range is greater, giving higher high tides and lower low tides. We refer to these as spring tides , which occur all year, not just in spring. When the sun, Earth and moon are at opposing angles we experience the smallest range between high and low tide. High low and low high tides are called 'neap' tides. It takes around seven days from spring to neap tide and then another seven days back again.

A good rule of thumb for a recreational kiteboarder is to learn the tides at your local beach at a specific time. For example, if it is high tide at midday on Saturday and this gives good tidal conditions, then two weeks later the tide will be similar, whereas the Saturday in between and the one after will be low tide at the same time of day.

When the tide is coming in it can be described as 'flooding', and when it is on its way out it is known as 'ebbing'. (See page 44 for more on the speed of this.)

Given that the Earth has a great amount of anomalies, such as landmass, this ebbing and flowing of the tide is far from regular the world over. Large bodies of water such as oceans often possess moderate tidal ranges and streams, whereas smaller seas and channels can boast some of the largest tidal ranges and strongest currents.

The Mediterranean Sea, for instance, has a very small tidal range of less than 0.5m (1.5ft) due to its large area and small opening to the ocean through the Gibraltar Strait, which does not allow enough time for it to empty and fill quickly enough to enable greater tidal range. The nearby English Channel, however, has very strong tidal influences and correspondingly increased range and flow. The reasons for this difference in range are down to physical factors in the area, with the topography, water depth, shoreline configuration, size of the ocean basin etc giving every location a slightly unique pattern. The area with the largest tidal range is the Bay of Fundy in Nova Scotia, which has a spring range of 11.5m (38.5ft), which would cover a normal two-storey house up to the chimney!

▼ Spring tides occur on the full and new moons where the gravitational forces of the sun and moon are aligned. Neap tides occur in the half moon phases of the lunar cycle when the gravitational forces of the sun and moon are opposed. This results in spring tides having high highs and low lows, and neap tides having moderate lows and moderate high waters.

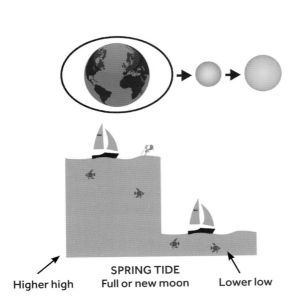

SPRING TIDE
Full or new moon
Higher high   Lower low

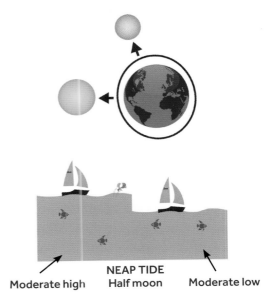

NEAP TIDE
Half moon
Moderate high   Moderate low

RULE OF TWELFTHS

The rising and falling of huge amounts of water creates some very fast-flowing streams or currents, which in turn can be both inconvenient and dangerous to kiteboarders. The 'point' of the tide, which incurs the fastest current, is the mid-point between high and low tide, on both the flooding and the ebbing tide.

At high water and at low water the flow momentarily stops, or 'stands'. As the water then begins to flood in or ebb out it gains momentum towards the middle two hours of the cycle, when up to 50 per cent of the water is moved in a third of the time. This can quickly turn underwater hazards into dangerous protruding obstacles and create currents with speeds of up to 10 knots at their peak.

The Rule of Twelfths is a simple way to understand and measure this flow during the tidal cycle. It separates the tidal range of water into 12 equal segments. In the first hour one-twelfth (or one 'segment') of the water is moved, the second hour moves two segments, and the third and fourth hours move three segments each. Hour five slows back down to two segments, leaving one remaining in the sixth hour.

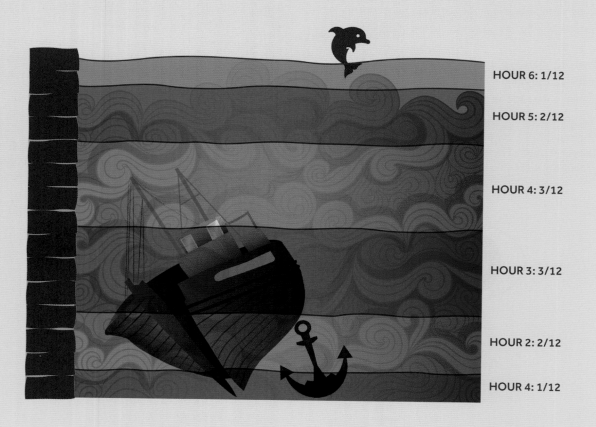

HOUR 6: 1/12

HOUR 5: 2/12

HOUR 4: 3/12

HOUR 3: 3/12

HOUR 2: 2/12

HOUR 4: 1/12

RIPS AND CURRENTS

The rise and fall of the tide is not the only thing that can create horizontal water flow. Rip tides are created by waves crashing tonnes of water on to a shoreline. This water has to find its way back into the sea and, like a river through a valley, it will quickly identify the path of least resistance and create a rip current, similar to a river, within the sea heading away from the beach.

A trained eye can identify these rips visually as they affect the breaking waveform. Kiteboarders can ride over a rip current dozens of times and barely notice it until a board or crashed kite is caught in one. The way to escape a rip current is to swim at 90 degrees to the flow to the edge of it, and as most of these are less than 50m (165ft) wide they are relatively easy to exit. The flow within a rip current increases with the size of the swell and subsequent quantity of water escaping seawards.

EFFECTS OF TIDES ON KITEBOARDERS

What do these tides mean for kiteboarders? Well firstly, most kite spots 'work' at a certain state of the tide, so planning your day to arrive at the right time is vital in order to avoid a long walk or disappointment. Occasionally, in certain locations such as river mouths, estuaries and channels, the tide can have a positive increasing effect upon the wind. If a westerly facing estuary has a 12 knot westerly wind blowing and an ebbing tide of 3 knots, the wind can appear to be 15 knots, making it easy to stay upwind and ride on a moderate-wind day. This is known as 'wind versus tide'. Six hours later the same location and wind can appear to be only 9 knots and it would be virtually impossible to stay upwind or ride at all. This is 'wind with tide' and is far less popular with kiteboarders.

All the effects and variations in tides can be planned, used and avoided by a smart kiteboarder to increase time on the water and prevent accidents and trouble occurring during a session. One of the most useful ways to get into these habits is to watch and talk to fellow kiteboarders at the beach who, in my experience, love to pass on their knowledge of and advice on the local dos and don'ts.

WATER STATES: MAKING WAVES

The surface state of the sea has a direct correlation to the strength and direction of the wind. A calm glassy morning on Turkey's summertime western Mediterranean coast can make the sea appear like a sheet of glass, while at sunset there are often small waves and a choppy sea courtesy of the afternoon sea breeze.

The state of the sea depends on the strength of the wind blowing across it and the length of the 'fetch' between landfalls. The friction of the wind at the water's surfaces

WHERE ARE TIDES MEASURED FROM AND WHO HAS THE INFO?

As with weather and wind data, tidal information is plentiful online, although sometimes it is easier and quicker to digest by referring to a local tide timetable available from a kite shop, marina or harbour office. Tides are measured in height from a level called 'chart datum', which is a calculated lowest-possible level that low tide can reach (although this is occasionally breached by extreme circumstances). The time is calculated at numerous ports and harbours around the world's coastlines. Be aware that this time can vary slightly at your local kite spot, but you can easily find out an accurate time by chatting to local kiteboarders.

creates tiny wavelets, which grow with the wind's strength. These are pulled down by gravity in a failing attempt to flatten out the surface of the water, but in actual fact serve to regulate the gaps between peaks and troughs and create waves. This choppy, chaotic sea grows in wave height and length with increasing wind and space up to around Beaufort Scale Force 10, which then counters the growing wave heights by blowing the tops off in mid-ocean and forcing them to break without their usual seabed catalyst.

Waves are measured in two ways. 'Height' is calculated from the trough of the swell to the adjacent peak. 'Period', or wave length, is measured from peak to peak. A long fetch, such as that of the Atlantic or Pacific, can help regulate the wave length as the swells collide and combine over distance. The height of a wave as it breaks upon a shoreline is culturally debated the world over and is the topic of many post-session beers.

These mid-ocean swells cannot only reach great heights, in excess of 30m (100ft) during strong storms, but they can also travel at up to 80kph (50mph) over open ocean, which is over 1,000km (620 miles) a day! Once they reach the coast the kinetic energy begins to connect with the seabed at around half their wave length in depth. This has a slowing effect on the wave at ground level, which allows the peak to continue faster than the base, resulting in the wave breaking and dissipating its energy on the shoreline. This also results in the height of the wave increasing as it meets the shoreline and seabed. Some waves can double in face height before they break on the shore. The longer the wave period the more it will increase in size as it reaches shallow water, which is why surfers not only look at the size of a swell, but also the period, which can often give a better-quality wave.

The angle and surface of the seabed dictates the way in which the wave above will break. A shallow-shelving

▼ **Wave propagation.**

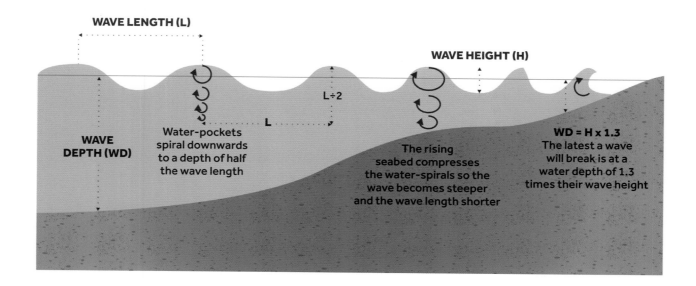

WAVE LENGTH (L)

WAVE HEIGHT (H)

L÷2

L

WAVE DEPTH (WD)

Water-pockets spiral downwards to a depth of half the wave length

The rising seabed compresses the water-spirals so the wave becomes steeper and the wave length shorter

WD = H x 1.3 The latest a wave will break is at a water depth of 1.3 times their wave height

sandy seabed will create a crumbling wave breaking gradually on to the shore. The opposite, which is searched for by surfers around the globe, is a steep rocky incline from deep water on to a shallow reef or shoreline. This creates a plunging and sometimes tubular wave, which every surfer (and the odd kiteboarder) dreams of getting inside for a moment of serenity with the ocean.

SEAS, OCEANS, RIVERS AND LAKES

The world boasts some incredibly diverse water environments for kiteboarders, thanks to the combination of travel becoming accessible to more and more of us and kiteboarding equipment being more compact than that of any other watersport. The coastal zones of Europe, the Americas, Australia, New Zealand and ever-increasingly Asia are becoming awash with resident and nomadic kiteboarders searching out flat shallow lagoons for freestyle and fiercely pitching waves for the kiteboarding fraternity. In addition, competitions have brought the sport more into the mainstream, with IKA course-racing World Cups being held in front of thousands of spectators in places such as Hong Kong, Italy and Egypt.

Temperatures around the world also differ hugely: from ice-breaking frigid water in the fjords of Iceland, Alaska and the poles – requiring neoprene protection from head to toe – to tropical bikini conditions along the equator and trade-wind belts. It is not only the coastlines that kiteboarding has taken by storm in the last decade however. The great lakes of North America and smaller inland waters from Texas to the Alpine mountains of Europe provide great kiteboarding conditions with consistent warm thermal winds during summertime, and even ice and snowkiting conditions in wintertime. Man-made trenches, such as the Lüderitz speed canal in Namibia, host annual wind speed competitions for windsurfers and kiteboarders in remote and harsh conditions.

The Hawaiian islands continue to be leaders in design innovation and seek to conquer some of the most challenging conditions on the planet. With temperate, year-round warm temperatures and very consistent wind statistics, it is home to many brands, world champions and some of the most famous spots such as Kite Beach and Ho'okipa Beach, which are the stomping grounds of the 'who's who' in the kiteboarding industry.

As these spots become overcrowded, the discovery of new wind Meccas – such as those found along Brazil's northeastern coastline and the shores that experience South Africa's Christmas Cape Doctor and Western Australia's southwest sea breeze – give a truly endless summer season to global kiteboarding. In addition, the manufacturing side of the industry has led to many new areas being popularised, with destinations from Sri Lanka to the Philippines being standard bucket-list tick boxes for the exploratory kiter today.

TIME ON THE WATER

Understanding this 'need to know' section of the book provides an essential and very useful foundation for your kiteboarding career, no matter what your discipline is within the sport. No one yet knows how many kiteboarding locations there are in the world – let's just say it's a lot, and growing every day. Knowing when to go out and when to stay on shore comes from a good attitude combined with a sound understanding of these factors. The combination of wind and water can produce everything from the valuable Venturi effect to dangerous turbulence, the wind vs. tide effect to the perilous conditions posed by the presence of hidden rocks beneath the water's surface.

Searching out the cross-shore side of an island at the right tidal state for the infamous reef-break to turn, or finding the hidden tidal lagoon at the right time can be hugely rewarding, keep you safe and simply increase the 'stoke' of being a kiteboarder. At the very least it can help you to arrive at the local beach when there's some wind, rather than waiting all morning for the sea breeze to kick in.

PART 2

The Journey:
Becoming A Kiteboarder

04

Getting started

Getting started

There are three main elements that will govern your learning experience of kiteboarding: the location, the equipment and you. If you get all of these elements right there will be no stopping you, or rather there will be, but in a controlled, planned fashion with a smile on your face after a safe, fun and informative session.

START WITH YOURSELF – HEALTH, SAFETY AND ATTITUDE

First, it is important to take a look at yourself to see if this is the sport for you. The 'extreme' label kiteboarding has gained is fully justified – as is true of the elite echelons of most modern sports today, which constantly strive to go faster, higher, further and break established records – but for your average person the experience can be far more moderate. Kiteboarding is in fact very accessible, and children from as young as six to veterans in their 80s can kiteboard. However, while you don't need to be in Ironman Triathlon-fitness condition or able to cycle a leg of the Tour de France to learn, a reasonable level of fitness and the ability to swim, both for beginners and when more advanced and heading out to sea, are a must. I describe these skills as water- and self-confidence.

Both aerobic and anaerobic energy is expanded while learning to kiteboard and then practising it, so it helps if you are fit. Being used to a bit of physical exertion, being able to take a couple of knocks and scrapes is part of learning any sport, and kiteboarding is no different. Taking care of yourself while you are learning is also fundamental, as trying too hard in extreme heat can bring down the fittest of people with sunburn, dehydration and exhaustion.

▼ Happy learners post-lesson.

SAFETY AT SEA

The intelligent kiteboarder is the one who can say, 'No, it's too much for me today', and wait for more suitable conditions, which often can be nearby or will occur after a few hours of watching and waiting for the wind to subside. I always apply this rule to my own watersports; if I cannot swim or rescue myself from a situation then I try not to put myself in it.

A good generic checklist of seaworthy advice, which I have adhered to over the years, comprises the 'seven common sense rules of the sea', summarised below:

1. Let someone know where you are going and when you plan to be back.
2. Go afloat with others, or at least make sure there is someone on the beach who can call for help.
3. Do good pre-flight checks on all your equipment and ensure that it is all sea- and flight-worthy.
4. Carry out a risk and site assessment, including getting a good weather and tidal forecast.
5. Avoid offshore winds, poor visibility, thunder and lightening, wind with tide, and fading light.
6. Be considerate to other water users (this includes having third-party insurance).
7. Don't over-exceed your own abilities when choosing a location.

▼ **Transferring the safety leash mid-lesson.**

As well as being in good general health, it is useful to have a positive attitude towards other people, both fellow kiteboarders and others using the beach or water. There are over 1.5 million kiteboarders in the world now, which is amazing. However, it means we can't get to know all of them that easily and for this reason we have developed some standard, universal signals, habits and behaviour that help us all to communicate more effectively, such as tapping one's head to signal that you need help to launch or land. Using these signals (see page 85), along with a bit of common sense and courtesy can really help things go smoothly at the beach, especially with so many kiteboarders coming from different countries and cultures and speaking different languages.

If all of these 1.5 million people stood in a line along a really, really long beach (imagine for a second) and each one had 30m (100ft) of space for their kites, then this line would stretch all the way around the world and once around Iceland's coastline to boot! This highlights the immense potential we have as a sport to occupy a vast amount of space, but also the dangerous impact that we could have upon a lot of people if things go wrong. Imagine the effect of dropping your kite and lines into a crowded surf line-up, or among a dinghy racing fleet in the harbour. There is a real responsibility to integrate positively with each other and other water- and beach-users if we want to maintain access to our favourite spots.

We will examine the more structured rules of the road, signals and etiquette in the second section of the book. Along with these a good, commonsense friendly attitude at the beach will not only make you friends and improve everyone's day, but could also be the prompt for someone to come to your aid if something breaks.

HOW, WHO AND WHERE TO LEARN

People always ask me 'How long does it take to learn?' or 'How hard is it?' These are difficult questions to answer as everyone learns at different speeds and some people learn easily, others with far more effort. A rough suggestion is to receive three to five days of tuition with good kit, instruction and conditions in order to give yourself a solid idea of the sport and how to progress. You may even manage to go riding along on the board during this time. To become independent and safe to go out on your own sometimes takes a little longer, and to become an intermediate or expert in the sport is a lifetime's challenge, which you will enjoy more and more as you progress because this is the most fun bit.

There is a definite formula for successful learning, which is set out in this chapter. Taking the steps in the correct order not only enhances the learning process but also sets a solid foundation for the future, whichever kiteboarding avenue you go down. Make sure you learn with the right people, in the right place and using the right kit. The culture of learning has progressed from the early days of large groups of friends learning together, towards small groups and one-to-one learning, which effectively speeds up the process to as rapidly as the individual can progress through the learning stages. Do some research, maybe even take a holiday to somewhere warm and windy where you can indulge in the learning experience for a week or two. Enjoy it, listen and have fun.

▲ No wind on the beach in the morning.   ▼ Windy beach in the afternoon.

The kite

The kite

There are many types, sizes and designs of kite, which are evolving all the time. For the purposes of this section, we will look at a small mid-aspect ratio foil kite flown on a bar with a functioning safety system.

BASIC POWERKITE-FLYING ON LAND

The assembly and rigging of these simple kites is both quick and easy with just two or perhaps three lines to connect and no real trimming systems. Your instructor can show you how the 'lark's head' (see page 60 for a diagram) or 'swan's neck' knot attaches the lines to the bridles of the kite. The kite must be secured on the ground so it doesn't blow away while you prepare it, and the bar and lines laid out and any twists removed.

Launching a small foil trainer kite in light winds is also straightforward. It requires the use of the 'thumbs-up' signal from both ends and for the launcher, who at this stage is likely to be the instructor, to hold the kite correctly. Depending on the wind conditions and the instructor's discretion the kite can be launched from the sides of the window at 9 o'clock or 3 o'clock, or from further into the window if the wind is weaker (see static wind window diagram on page 28).

Once the kite is launched, you need to gain control of the kite in the neutral zone, holding the kite at 9 o'clock or 3 o'clock. These points are used for launching, landing, resting and putting the board on. Generating power should be learned gradually by trying out a small figure-of-eight pattern back and forth above the pilot's head. As you gain in confidence, the size and positivity of this shape can be increased using the bar. This pattern is great fun to practise on land but is not as useful on water as it generates power straight downwind, which is rarely a good direction in sailing terms.

The sequence of images opposite (diving the kite) shows how we can generate power and speed with the kite through the intermediate zone in a certain direction. This requires quick and positive bar steering by the pilot, as only half of the window is being used at one time. This is the motion used by everyone from beginners to experts to get up and going on the board in the water, and the smoother and more precise the pattern the better the results.

Moving with the kite on land and understanding the effect this has on the kite is also very beneficial. Practising the pattern outlined above while walking across the wind in the correct direction simulates kiteboarding on water. Travelling upwind and holding the kite in the neutral zone also helps a beginner return to their start point. Flying

Steering/diving a kite in a 'sine wave' pattern to generate power in one direction.

the kite with one hand, holding the board and twisting and untwisting the lines are all great exercises to perfect, and greatly aid future progression.

LEI RIGGING AND ASSEMBLY

Rigging up your kite is a fundamental skill to acquire, and you need to get it right every time you go kiteboarding; there is no room for error when it comes to the correct assembly process.

Modern kites all rig better with the bar downwind. There are a number of reasons for this, but primarily it is so that the kite is not in the power zone, and the bridles can be viewed as intended to fly. It's good to create your own routine so you follow a plan each time. Usually it's best to inflate and position the kite on the beach first, in the secure position. Be sure it's sufficiently pumped to the manufacturer's recommendation for psi pressure and that the struts are locked if it's a one-pump system. Always put something on top of the kite to prevent it from flying away, such as some sand, the board, the harness, your spouse...

Unwind your lines downwind from the kite and lay the bar following the 'Red on the Right for Rigging' motto for

rigging. You can put some sand on them or wrap them around your board handle to prevent them following you downwind if the breeze is strong. Walk up the lines removing any tangles; you can do this twice with a 5-line kite to get the outsides correct first, and then worry about the insides.

Once the lines are laid out and tangle-free, attach them to the correct positions on the kite: outside lines to the back edges, and central lines to the front. Many manufacturers colour-code the knots to help you get this process right. Connect all lines with a lark's head knot.

▲ Kites must be stowed on the beach and secured with sand or your board. The leading edge should be to the wind and lines trailing downwind. It's good etiquette to wrap these up as in the picture to reduce tangles on the beach.

LARK'S HEAD KNOT

Coming from a sailing and scouting background yet being consistently hopeless at tying knots, I find it incredibly reassuring that every single kite in any of these generic categories uses exactly the same knot to connect the lines to the bridles or directly to the kite.

The lark's head – also known as the swan's neck, lark's foot, slipknot or even the cow hitch – dates back centuries and is a true work of genius. It takes five seconds to learn, five seconds to do, holds through even the windiest and strenuous sessions, and can be undone in five seconds. It's far easier to show how to do knots than talk through them, so here's an illustration of my, and every kiteboarder's, favourite.

PRE-FLIGHT CHECKS

Before asking a friend or fellow kiteboarder to launch you, double-check your lines by tracing down the outside lines visually from the kite to the bar. This serves to prevent problems once in the launch position.

LAUNCHING AN LEI KITE

Once a good grasp of the wind window has been gained using a foil kite, the next stage in the learning process is to harness and control an LEI kite, which I will refer to as 'tube' kites from now on. These are by far the most common type used, and are explained in full in the equipment section.

Launching the kite is one of the most important skills to master as a beginner, and is a technique you will need to employ every single time you go kiteboarding in the future. Fortunately, there is a really easy and fundamentally safe way to launch a kite anywhere in the world, and if you follow the simple steps every time you go to the beach you will never create an issue. Successful launching begins with the correct pre-flight checked assembly of your kite before you get into the launch position; it is really important to ensure none of the lines have been tangled or incorrectly attached during the rigging procedure.

Before you ask the classic kiteboarding chat-up line 'can you launch my kite?', think through where you and the kite need to be positioned. Once you have got into the right place, the first thing to do when you pick up your bar is to attach your leash; this ensures that you are safely connected to your kite from the earliest opportunity. I always do this before looking at my launching assistant, as this prevents any visual miscommunications that they may construe as being a signal to launch. If you have correctly rigged your kite with the bar downwind you can walk towards the launching position with no power in the kite's canopy.

Once you are positioned across the wind with your kite-launching assistant holding your kite in the correct position you can then tension the lines and possibly walk a few paces towards the wind to ensure the whole canopy is tensioned and ready for take off. If any part of the canopy is flapping, or any of the lines are slack, then the kite will not take off and launch properly. Once you can feel some tension in the lines, it is your job as the pilot to

🔺 **Bar and safety leash correctly attached.**

double-check that your safety system, bar trimming and lines are all correct as far as you can see.

From the kite launcher's perspective it is important to know how to hold the kite in the correct position, standing upwind of the kite holding the leading edge in the centre by the inflation valve. Once the kite has some power and is not flapping it is the launcher's job to visually check the bridles as far as they can see. Once the pilot and the kite launcher have checked their respective ends, they can individually signal a thumbs-up to one another. Once both people have signalled the thumbs-up the kite can be released and raised slowly up the side of the window towards the neutral position by the pilot. NEVER LAUNCH A KITE WITHOUT TWO THUMBS-UP.

KEY POINTS:

- Pre-flight check your kit before getting into the launching position.
- Brief your kite-launching partner on signals, kite-checking and how to release the kite,
- Always make sure there is a thumbs-up signal from both ends before launching any kite.

1 Signal to a willing landing assistant.

2 Landing assistant grabs the kite by the leading edge and walks towards the pilot.

3 Landing assistant secures the kite on the beach.

It is important to weigh down the kite with sand, bar or board to prevent it taking off and blowing down the beach.

LANDING AN LEI KITE

As with launching, landing the kite is all about communication, which can be very effectively done using the international 'land my kite signal' of tapping your head, demonstrated here in Step 1 opposite. In addition to using the signal, eye contact between the pilot and landing partner is required. Once you have identified and communicated with your landing partner it is then the pilot's job to gauge his/her landing spot in relation to the landing partner. It is good etiquette for the pilot to manoeuvre him/herself as much as is practical to minimise the distance a helpful landing partner has to travel on the beach. Make sure that the descending kite is not travelling too quickly towards the ground in order to avoid a crash-landing and, once at ground level, hover the kite so your landing partner can easily grab and secure it. As soon as the landing partner has taken hold of the kite, it is very helpful if the pilot steps towards the kite to remove the tension in the lines.

As the pilot it is your job to go and secure the kite in the safety position and make sure it is weighted down correctly before undertaking any other tasks, but your landing partner may offer to do it. Ensuring the kite is anchored is a key skill and a common request whenever you are down the beach, and it is also a great way to interact, help, keep the beach safe and get to know your local kiteboarding community.

KEY POINTS:

- Signal and engage in communications with the landing partner.
- Bring the kite down slowly, keep control, and hover it at ground level.
- As soon as the kite is in a secure position the pilot's job is to ensure the kite and lines are not endangering or inconveniencing other people or kiteboarders on the beach.

▲ **Crosswind powered body-drag.**

BODY-DRAGGING

The basic reason for learning to body-drag is to gain control, power, direction and stability from a kite in water. This is not only great fun to do but will hugely increase your confidence levels with the kite, which can be fairly non-existent at first. While learning to body-drag it is not uncommon to crash the kite, which is why launching, landing, relaunching and self-rescue are also taught during a beginner's first water sessions.

There are a few ways to teach body-dragging and techniques differ around the world in relation to environments and wind conditions. I have outlined the common body-drags here, which allow a beginner to gradually build their ability and technique by generating power first, then the ability to move in the right direction, retrieve their board and put it on. In the same way that a surfer needs to be good at paddling, a proficient kiteboarder needs to master and perfect these body-dragging skills.

POWER: DOWNWIND FIGURE-OF-EIGHT BODY-DRAGGING

The key to generating power with the kite is to fly it into the power-zone area that resides directly downwind of the pilot, in the centre of the wind window.

Kneel down or float on your front with your legs behind you. Then, starting with the kite in the neutral position at 12 o'clock, begin generating power by steering the kite gradually from left to right in a small figure-of-eight pattern above and in front of you. As you gain confidence and control the kite can be steered more positively from side to side, sweeping across the power zone about halfway up in the window. Be sure to turn the kite before it reaches the neutral zones on either side.

Once mastered this is not only a fun exercise, but also serves to generate power in the kite that can be used to travel from A to B in a downwind or dead-run direction.

KEY POINTS:

- **Begin by kneeling or floating on your front with your legs behind you.**
- **Execute a small figure-of-eight pattern to start generating power, then increase the size of the figure-of-eight gradually.**
- **Once moving, keep the bar sheeted in to produce positive tension and steerage in the back lines.**
- **To stop, steer the kite to 12 o'clock and allow it to ascend to a stop, sheeting out the bar at the same time.**

▼ **Downwind body-drag.**

1 Sheet in and steer the kite from side to side across the window in front of you.

2 Turn positively before the kite reaches the side of the window.

3 Fly back across the window.

4 Repeat the steering back and forth as necessary.

DIRECTION: CROSSWIND BODY-DRAGGING

The next step is to generate both power and direction. When kiteboarding a rider will travel to the left (port tack) or to the right (starboard tack). This pattern is used frequently and it serves to generate initial power to rise up on to the board from the board-start position. It is also used to increase power and speed if a rider slows down in a lull (a brief localised drop in wind speed).

The technique to master with crosswind body-dragging is to only use the right side of the wind window when travelling to the right (starboard), and vice versa. The pilot should start with the kite at 12 o'clock and initiate a positive dive in the desired direction. The kite needs to descend reasonably vertically in order to generate power, and it then needs to be positively redirected to ascend upwards back towards 12 o'clock. This sine-wave pattern can be executed positively up and down for the desired distance. To stop, the pilot can direct the kite upwards to 12 o'clock and let the bar out.

A reasonable angle to drag through the water is 45 degrees across and downwind.

This is the exact pattern a kiteboarder uses to get up and going on a kite, so the more you master it now, the easier you will find riding when you get on to the board.

▼ **Crosswind powered body-drag.**

1 Kite on side of window you wish to travel.

2 Kite diving to produce directional power.

3 Kite redirected upwards positively remaining in the power/intermediate area of the window continuing to generate power.

4 Kite ascending in the power/intermediate zone towards the zenith/12 o'clock.

RETRIEVING THE BOARD: BODY-DRAGGING WITH/BACK TO THE BOARD

Now you have produced both power and directional power with the kite you need to make sure you can retrieve your board when you fall off, which is inevitable during the learning process, and likely to occur at some point even when you can perform advanced tricks. Grasping this board-retrieval body-drag skill is fundamental to sustainable kiteboarding and allows you more time on the board and less time chasing it!

Unlike the previous two body-drags, the board-retrieval drag doesn't involve moving the kite or generating power; it is about generating stability and an efficient angle across the wind. The kite should be flown to one side in the neutral zone, at either 10–11 o'clock or 1–2 o'clock. You need to control the kite with your top hand.

The other hand should be pointing in the direction of travel. The whole body needs to be as straight as possible to slice through the water like a fin, across wind and maybe a little bit upwind. The bar should be mobile, allowing the kite to 'breathe', giving a small amount of backline tension but not over-sheeting or causing the kite to stall.

▼ **Body-dragging back to and with the board is a key skill to learn.**

KEY POINTS:

- **Fly the kite with one hand, half sheeted in, on the side of the window you wish to travel in. The higher the kite is the better, as this avoids it falling into the water in light airs.**
- **Point your lower arm in the direction of travel (not towards the board) and try to make your body straight like a fin, so you can slice through the water efficiently.**
- **Trust the theory that your board will drift downwind to you. Count to ten as you drag, then slowly turn and re-count to ten – I bet your board will magically appear!**

You can also execute this drag while carrying the board, for instance if you needed to get out into the water through a shore-break, or in order to travel to a safe area to board start. Use the same technique as before – simply hold the board with your front hand, either by the handle or front footstrap.

BALANCE (STABILITY AND CONTROL): THE BALANCE-DRAG

You can now generate power and direction and are able to retrieve the board. All you have to do now is get on your feet in a controlled way using the balance-drag, and prepare for the board start. Just like body-dragging with the board, the balance-drag is a controlled drag, not a powered one.

Put the kite at 12 o'clock and lie on your back, looking up at the kite with either one or two hands on the moderately sheeted bar. Try to float your feet out in front of you and lean your shoulders and head back. Identify something directly downwind of you and try to keep a foot either side of it. Use your whole body to try to keep you stable and facing downwind, getting used to flying the kite with one hand and using all your limbs. The purpose of this drag is to create some equilibrium

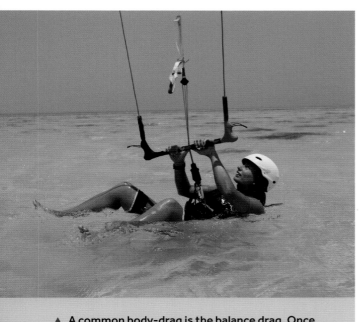

🔺 **A common body-drag is the balance drag. Once mastered this allows the board to be put on your feet with ease.**

before you handle the board. The kite remains the key factor at this stage and if it is kept under control it will allow the board to slip on easily. If you are very tense and not in control of the kite it is likely to crash once you reach for the board.

KEY POINTS:

- **Keep the kite in the neutral zone above you at 12.30–1.30 o'clock.**
- **Lean back, look at the kite and bring your hips up to make your body as wide and flat as possible – like a starfish.**
- **RELAX if you feel yourself twisting; use your arms and legs to help reposition yourself. Correct twists early on in order to maintain the position.**

RELAUNCHING A KITE

In the last few years, it has become infinitely easier to relaunch a kite. Advances in modern kite design mean they can be safely relaunched in a controlled manner in a matter of seconds. This helps build a progressing kiteboarder's confidence and allows you to try new things safe in the knowledge that if the kite crashes it will fly again easily, allowing you to carry on enjoying your session.

There are some generic guidelines for all inflatable kites, and then some more specific tips for different more specialist kites. Here we look at the two most common types of relaunch for 4-line and 5-line kites.

HYBRID 4-LINE KITES

Most modern hybrid kites fly on a simplistic front-line bridle system and non-geared rear steering lines, so we will first look at how you get this type of kite to go up if it hits the deck.

First, allow the kite to fill with wind so the canopy is producing some pull, and position it downwind of the pilot with all or part of the leading edge lying on the surface of the water. Choose the logical or preferred side to launch and take hold of the rear steering line on the opposing side – ie use the right-hand line to launch to the left and the left-hand line to launch to the right.

Hold the line, without wrapping it around your hand, about 30–40cm (12–16in) up the line. The top of the float is often a good place. Hold this still without pulling or jabbing at the line, to create tension. This will result in the kite turning on to its side as it travels slowly towards the edge of the wind window. Control the speed by feathering the line as this happens, being careful not to pull too much line as this will result in the kite falling backwards on to its trailing edge and the pilot having to start the process again.

Once the kite is approaching the neutral zone or is in the intermediate zone, transfer your hand on to the

bar from the line and steer the kite up the side of the window to 12 o'clock, in the same way as you would for an assisted launch.

KEY POINTS:

- Let the kite assume its intended shape downwind in the window.
- Hold the desired sideline still to create controlled tension as the kite travels to the side of the window.
- Transfer your hand on to the bar before the kite leaves the water. Steer it up the neutral zone in control, in the same way as you would for an assisted launch.

5-LINE KITES: 5TH-LINE RELAUNCH

The invention of the 5th line in 2005 initially helped C-shaped kites to turn on to their side and speeded up the relaunch process, especially in light winds. The method used is the same as for 4-line kites and really helps bigger kites in lighter winds. The basic principle is that pulling about 1m (3ft) of the 5th line in at the bar end angles the centre of the canopy in such a way that wind can flow over it, allowing the kite to turn more efficiently on to one side and begin travelling towards the side of the window. Since 2016, 5-line kites have been losing popularity, whereas the majority of 4-line bridled kites can launch as easily by holding the upper front line in the same manner. The bridles allow the kite to travel towards the side of the wind window more easily, and the lack of the extra line reduces inversion tangles with the lines.

Bars, or 'control systems' as they are often referred to nowadays, are governed by an ISO standard that was

◀ Pull the 5th line to get the kite to come onto its side and travel to the side of the window quicker. Retracting the 5th line then allows the kite to take its standard shape and launch normally.

5th-line relaunch.

1 Pull a full arm's length of 5th line to roll the kite onto its back/side.

2 Get the top wing tip to tension and begin to pull the kite upright and towards the side of the window.

3 As the kite stands up and moves to the edge of the window, slowly retract the 5th line.

4 With the 5th line almost retracted, tension the topline slightly to encourage it to launch.

5 Continue to slightly tension the topline and wait for bottom wing tip to release from the water's surface.

6 Steer up the side of the window towards 12 o'clock.

The board

06

The board

A kiteboard is a vital piece of equipment, and its size, volume and type can all have an impact on the ride as well as determining who can use it. Windsurfers always refer to their boards with a volumetric measurement. Kiteboarders are beginning to quote this measurement more and more for foiling type boards, as this gives an indication of its flotation. Directional surfboards will also quote a volume as well as length and width. This helps a rider choose the right board, depending on their weight and skill level. Twin tips have negligible buoyancy, hence are judged more on their length, width and construction makeup.

HOW THE BOARD WORKS

Although there is a great range of board types within kiteboarding, all (bar foils), are governed by the same laws in terms of motion. Kiteboarding is primarily a planing sport. Planing occurs when a board or craft skims across the surface of the water in front of its own bow wave. The minimum and maximum planing speed depends on the size, volume and shape of the board: bigger boards will plane earlier and smaller ones later.

Planing generally starts when the board or craft is moving at a speed upwards of 10 knots. To get on to the plane, reasonable amounts of force and momentum are required to rise over the board's bow wave and support the rider's weight. Think of a speedboat rising out of the water on to the plane; you can often feel a resistance point and hear the engine change as it rises over the 'stagnation point'. This usually requires most or all of the engine power, yet

once the boat is up the throttle will be reduced (hopefully) as the resistance decreases, meaning the craft will continue accelerating.

In technical terms, as the board gains in speed it produces increasing amounts of lift. This is proportional to the angle of attack and the speed of the craft squared. In the simplest terms, the faster you go the better and the more weight you can support. This is why you can see some big people waterskiing, surfing and kiteboarding on boards that would not support them at all in displacement mode.

Displacement mode is how a cargo ship or large ferry travels through water. They push water around their hull shape, which displaces an amount of water as it travels. These vessels don't have enough power to get on to the plane, thank goodness, as planing oil tankers is a scary concept! It could be argued that small people on large volume boards can maintain a displacement mode for prolonged periods, without sinking, due to the extra volume and width of the boards.

These laws directly relate to us when we are kiteboarding. If we don't have enough power or wind, we sometimes can't get on to the plane or rise the board over the stagnation point on to its bow wave, or stay there once planing. A kiteboarder would refer to this as 'underpowered'. Too much wind and then speed creates too much lift and force, which becomes uncontrollable. This is referred to as 'overpowered'.

There is a third dimension to how the board works once you are planing. This is called 'lateral resistance', and is created by the fins gripping and creating resistance against you, the rider, pushing against them. The result is forwards motion across the wind, the angle of which can be changed from a beam to broad reach by you altering your stance and foot pressure, which in turn changes the angle of attack of the board and consequently its direction.

Edging against the rail of a board can also produce grip and resistance. This is done when the rail of the board is applied at an angle to the water by digging in your heels once planing, which can have as much or more effect than the fins on certain boards.

The resistance caused by the fins is primarily a good thing as it lets the board grip and steer. Any resistance creates drag as a by-product, so fin design has become extremely important for racing boards, since at full speed the board can be completely above the water with the fins doing all the work. This has been taken to the extreme with hydrofoiling, a sport in which the fin is ridden for prolonged periods, with the board being there simply to provide a standing platform.

GETTING ON THE BOARD

This is it, the moment you have been waiting for... The board start is a culmination of all the kite skills learned so far, which if they have been mastered successfully will make getting up on the board far easier and more controllable. Making sure you have a suitable kite, board, location and breeze makes getting up on the board infinitely easier too.

Before you attempt to get the board on your feet in the water, make sure you have adjusted the footstraps to your feet, so you can fit them in and can then control the board effectively by angling your feet. Also think about which direction you would prefer to come up in first. We are all 'wired' in one direction: 'regular' or 'goofy'. Regular is to the left 'port tack' with your left leg leading, goofy is with your right foot leading.

Pick a spot where there is plenty of space and keep a good look out for surrounding kiteboarders. Once you are in the balance-drag position with your board, control the kite with your preferred hand and hold the board with the other. Position the board in front of you and put the opposing foot to the hand holding the board into the strap, eg if your right hand is on the board then put the left foot in the strap first.

A really useful top tip here is to fly the kite on the side of the window that the board is on. So if you put your right foot in first, positioning the kite at 11 o'clock will help to push you towards the board rather than pull you away from it. Let go with your hand and drift towards the board, making sure you keep the kite above you and that you don't power it up. Once you have both feet on the board, raise the kite to 12 o'clock and work your feet securely into the straps. Take a moment to relax.

STANDING UP

Once you're secured on the board you will be quite steady. Bring the kite to 12 o'clock and decide which way you are going to try to come up first; most people prefer coming up to the right initially ('regular'). If this is the case then move the kite back to 11.30 o'clock in the neutral zone. This will allow for a more effective dive and also opens up your body to the direction of desired travel. Don't worry too much about the board direction on your first dive. The key is to dive the kite gently, and lean your body forwards with bent legs and your shoulders as far forwards as possible.

A reasonable goal to aim for at your first attempt is simply to get your bum out of the water without flying too far forwards.

Once you have got the technique of rolling up so you are over the board and moving slowly forwards then you can begin working on the board direction, standing up and starting to cover some distance.

KEY POINTS:

- Get the board on slowly and in control, paying attention to the kite and not powering it up.
- Start with small dives and lean your body forwards. Get your body weight over the board and stay low until you're up and balanced.
- Control your power and speed and enjoy the ride!

▼ **Getting board on, up and going.**

1 Kite and board on the same side of the window allow you to be pushed towards the board while putting your feet into the straps.

2 Once both feet are in, wedge and secure them and relax into this board start position.

3 Lean forward with your legs bent and your shoulders forward as you come up out of the water and start moving along the board.

4 Begin to extend the body into the correct stance and start edging across the wind from the broad reach direction travelled during the 'get up'.

THE FIRST RUN

It is not uncommon in the beginning to sink back down and stop on your first attempt. However, once you're coming up in control, start pointing the board forwards and towards the kite during the dive. Once you are up, keep the kite moving in the sine-wave pattern – similar to that used for the crosswind body-drag. Begin to apply some pressure (edging) to the heel side of the board and direct the board across the wind rather than just following the kite.

KEY POINTS:

- Keep the kite moving steadily in the direction of travel.
- Point the board and look towards where you want to go.
- Lean back to apply heel-edge pressure and put the weight through your harness.

▲ Riding comfortably.

STOPPING AND BASIC TURNING

STOPPING

Think about how far you want to go and identify a stopping or turning point. To slow down and control your speed, stop moving the kite in the sine-wave pattern and allow it to slowly ascend to 12 o'clock while sheeting the bar out to reduce the rear-line tension.

Once you are slowing down you can easily sit back down in the water into the board-start position. Prepare to travel in the other direction. Sticking your bum in the water is a great way to create resistance and acts like a brake, bringing you to a controlled stop quickly.

TURNING (THE SITTING GYBE)

To go back in the other direction, simply repeat the board-start technique in the opposite direction. Often this can feel a bit uncomfortable as we always have a dominant direction, which we usually start with. This is described as the 'sitting gybe'. A top tip for getting going 'goofy' is to point the board very broad downwind as this will help it come up forwards rather than snowploughing with your heels.

The more comfortable and confident you get, the quicker you will be able to slow down, sit and then take off in the new direction. Once you have mastered the basic sit-down turn, it is time to increase the speed and kite movement to keep your bum dry and slide the board around the turn while still standing. This is called the 'training gybe'.

The entry for a training gybe is exactly the same as for a sitting gybe, except you need to carry a little bit more speed. The primary difference is the kite movement, as this must be more positive through 12 o'clock and on to the new tack. It might take a few attempts to get the power level right, but once mastered this allows you to stay upright and dry all day long riding back and forth... Awesome!

KEY POINTS:

- Plan your turning spot and check around you for other riders.
- Slow down and carve hard into the wind. Move the kite positively and high through 12 o'clock and into the new direction of travel.
- Try to get your body weight over the board as you push the back leg forwards, pointing the board on to a very broad reach on the new tack.
- As you begin travelling in the new direction, begin carving and edging the board across the wind again.

▼ **The sitting gybe first run.**

1 Edge upwind to slow your speed and sit back into the harness while rising the kite to 12 o'clock.

2 Sit down into the water slowly with the kite at 12 o'clock.

3 Turn to face the new direction while in the board-start position and begin to dive the kite in the new direction.

4 Head on a broad reach in the new direction as you come up from the water leaning forward as in a standard board start.

5 Begin to edge and extend the body into your normal riding stance and direction across the wind.

AVOIDING ACCIDENTS

Often a hot topic before the first kiteboarding lesson even starts, accidents are something that can worry beginners. During the early experimental days of kiteboarding, when equipment evolution was progressing faster than skill levels or safety system technology, there were some accidents and, unfortunately, fatalities. But, as with Formula One motor racing, people learned very quickly that safety must come first, and equipment has to be fitted with the correct release systems and design characteristics to prevent uncontrollable flying errors occurring in the future. Today, safe equipment design and structured teaching schemes are much in evidence around the world, and these prevent a huge percentage of accidents.

Saying that, of course some accidents do happen, but they are rare and almost never occur in a learning environment. I separate and educate on accidents in two ways:

1 Accidents caused by kit or pilot error resulting in an incident occurring, eg bad launching, site assessment or decision making over the personal level and prevailing conditions.
2 Accidents incurred by individuals pushing the limits at the extreme end of their level, eg torn tendons, twisted ankles, knees and shoulders etc. When you push sport limits, sometimes the limits push back!.

Human error is the most common cause of modern kiteboarding accidents, and can include going out in slightly too much wind, with slightly too big a kite, at slightly too high tide, or not properly checking the lines before raising a thumb to launch. All these little errors can lead to a negative experience, but adopting a sensible and methodical rigging and launching process will keep you safe, as they have kept me, and everyone I have ever launched, since the beginning. So the golden rules are take your time, be honest about your own ability level in relation to the prevailing conditions on the day, think sensibly, and double-check kit, and nothing will go wrong.

The second type of accident occurs as a result of an attitude and is almost inevitable in the higher levels of kiteboarding, or any other sport, when risk-taking is required to push the boundaries. That said, the best athletes are often the ones who have avoided injury by being rigorously professional in their outlook and practices. Avoiding accidents is as easy in kiteboarding as in any sport, and with a bit of common sense and a good attitude these will not feature in your kiteboarding career.

RULES OF THE ROAD

Kiteboarding is a sail sport and follows a set of generic collision-avoidance rules common to all sail sports. These rules have been cemented and pressure tested in recent years due to the sport's inclusion as an Olympic class, and the very structured formats of racing it now displays within this genre of sport. It also has a unique three-dimensional format that gives rise to a few extra considerations. There are two types of collision-avoidance techniques: common-sense rules, which include respecting local culture and etiquette and generally being sensible; and structured sailing rules, which are used in racing, competitions and crowded areas. A good understanding of both and a positive approach to your own riding will keep you tangle-free. Remember, the purpose of all types of collision regulation is to avoid crashes at all costs.

COMMON-SENSE RULES

Launching and landing

Most beaches have an area where people can rig up. For convenience this may be by the car park, or if the location is a crowded, smaller beach then rigging up may be restricted to a specific area in order to prevent

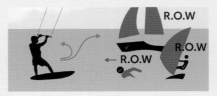

Other water users, right of way (R.O.W).

kite lines causing issues with others. If there is such an area, use it, as it is probably there for a reason. Huge beaches are less of a problemand it is generally easier to find a bit of your own space.

Jumping

Everyone loves to jump when kiteboarding. It is truly amazing and the airtime is endless compared to other watersports, especially on windy days. Be sure to give yourself enough space to land, regain control and not endanger yourself or others. Two kite lengths from anything downwind is a minimum distance to use as a guide, and this length increases by multiples upwards as your jumps grow. (Lewis Crathern cleared about 10–12 kite lengths when he jumped Brighton Pier.)

Looking before you turn

Not doing this is a classic cause of non-serious tangles at congested spots and is completely avoidable. We check around us when in a car or on a bicycle before pulling out at a junction, so do the same while kiteboarding. Take a glance behind you before redirecting your kite and you will avoid that embarrassing surprise and consequent swim. Likewise, try not to pen someone in and restrict him or her from turning. Doing so is a classic sailing racing trick, but it is a very antisocial and sometimes dangerous habit for leisure kiters on a busy beach. Doing it will not make you any friends either.

Planning and proximity

As well as looking before you turn, plan manoeuvres such as jumping, turning and riding a wave downwind. Erratic changes of direction and sudden moves can cause collisions and confusion. Relax, take your time and, if in doubt, give yourself extra space.

Local rules and cultures

Some specific locations can be unique and may have developed local habits and cultural etiquette. These may in your view be right or wrong, but they are hard to change and should be adhered to. An example could be a Brazilian lagoon where the 'trick spot' is on the left if looking from upwind. Often an order develops among the riders, who come in on port tack, perform a trick and then ride out downwind on starboard. This reverses the port-starboard rule perfectly safely and for a logical reason, and you would be wise to follow suit to avoid causing confusion or aggravation.

STRUCTURED RULES

Upwind kite up/downwind kite down

When out kiteboarding, it is common for kiteboarders to pass close to one another. As the two riders converge, the one closer to the wind must raise their kite, allowing the rider further downwind to pass easily underneath with their kite kept lower.

Rider in the water.

If the two approaching riders are on a collision course and are both at the same level to the wind, then the rider on the starboard tack (travelling right) has the priority to continue on this course, while the rider on the port tack (travelling left) must lower their kite and bear downwind to avoid a collision.

Overtaking

If two riders are on the same tack travelling in the same direction, the rider overtaking has the responsibility to keep clear as they pass.

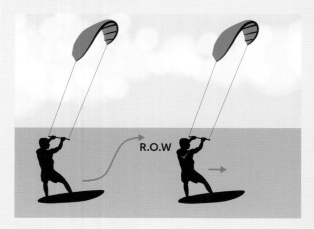

The sequence of images below shows how overtaking should happen.

1 The overtaking kiter raises their kite as they approach to pass.

2 The overtaking kiter keeps their kite high and steady, while the overtaken kiter remains on course.

3 Both maintain course until suitably clear from each other.

Rght of way

Windward board keeps clear of leeward board. This rule refers to the rider closest to the wind needing to not impede a rider below them, or to leeward. The reason for this is the leeward rider might not be aware of the windward rider, where being upwind enables vision and awareness of those downwind.

Leaving the beach

A kiter leaving the beach has right of way over one coming in. This is because a kiter just stepping on to their board in the shallows is closer to hazards on the beach, and may not have as much power or control as they head out through the shore-break. Someone wanting to come in should turn and take another run.

Exactly when a kiter has gained full momentum and is no longer 'leaving the beach' is a bit of a grey area that is much debated. The best advice here is to be considerate in both circumstances, as a collision aids neither party. I always try to avoid sections of the beach where there is a good breaker on the way out for two reasons: first, it's more likely to break on you; and second, there may be someone riding it. If you are riding a twin-tip and not trying to ride along the waves it is advisable not to go in the wavy area of a reef at all as you could dramatically obstruct the flow of kiters riding the waves.

Waveriding and reef breaks

Wave spots tend to be confusing places as kiters suddenly start travelling in very different directions. I am going to separate this into two scenarios:

1   A defined reef break with a peak, peeling-wave channel. On such a spot a pattern or order will usually develop, whereby a rider comes on to the wave upwind, rides along the wave travelling generally downwind as they do so, and kicks off the bottom of the wave before riding close-hauled out to sea downwind of the breaking wave and out of the way of the next waverider. This system works well if everyone sticks to the order and there are not too many people on the wave. The rider on the wave in this instance has right of way and no kiter should try to ride straight out through the breaking part of the wave, as this would potentially obstruct the waverider, who may not be able to stop if they are committing to the waves-breaking pattern.

2   A long beach with waves rolling in all along it and with launching potential throughout. This set-up is a bit of a melting pot, but it is generally the waverider who has right of way when they are on a wave and riding. However, if a person is leaving the beach and heading out, or has ridden in turned and is now riding out, they may not be able to avoid the waverider if they are not yet planing and waves are rolling towards them, in which case the waverider must avoid them.

COMMUNICATIONS AND SIGNALS

The combination of wind and a forced 25m (82ft) distance between the pilot and the kite makes speaking or shouting difficult. For this reason, signals are a brilliant way of communicating quickly and clearly, and enable kiteboarders to safely launch, land, ride and enjoy the sport together.

LAUNCHING

Always try to pick a fellow kiteboarder when launching and be polite and patient. Remember that it is ultimately the pilot's responsibility to ensure the launch goes safely, not the launching helper's. Once ready to launch the pilot should signal a 'thumbs-up' to the launcher. This gesture is saying 'I am attached correctly and can see my lines, bar and kite are all ready to go'. The launcher should return communications with a reciprocal thumbs-up, indicating 'the kite feels ready to launch and the bridles and lines are all correct at the kite end'.

The launcher should take special care to check the rear-line points to ensure the line is not caught around the tube or wing tip, as this is difficult to see or feel from the pilot's end.

◀ **Brazilian lagoon twin tippery.**

▲ **Launching.**

▲ Abort launch/land.

ABORT LAUNCH/DO NOT LAUNCH

To halt a launching kite, the signal used is a flat palm facing the launcher, indicating they should wait before releasing the kite. Removing hands from the bar also signifies a lack of readiness to launch.

LANDING

Kiteboarding's most commonly used signal is a pilot tapping his or her head while looking at a fellow kiteboarder. This means 'can you land my kite?'. The landing partner can also use this signal to indicate to the pilot they are willing to land the kite.

EJECT/RELEASE THE SAFETY

More commonly used by instructors, pushing both hands from the waist outwards together, exposing the palms, means 'release the safety system'.

▲ Landing.

▲ Eject/release the safety.

HELP/DISTRESS

Kiteboarders can use the international SOS signal of waving crossed arms above their head in the direction of anyone they wish to help them.

This means 'I am in need of urgent assistance. Please help'.

GO RIGHT /GO LEFT

Pointing both arms to the right or left, often used by an instructor while teaching, means 'please travel in the direction indicated'.

KITE TO 12 O'CLOCK

Forming a point with two hands pointing upwards means 'put the kite at 12 o'clock and stop'.

COME TO ME

An instructor can sometimes use the signal of one hand on their head with fingers pointing downwards to signal 'come to me'.

▲ Help/distress.

▲ Go right.   ▲ Go left.

▲ Kite to 12 o'clock.

▲ Come to me.

Safety,
breakages and
self-rescues

Safety, breakages and self-rescues

Watersports are practised on a dynamic platform – oceans, seas, rivers, lakes and estuaries – all of which change throughout the day with the tide (if applicable), and over the seasons. What can be shallow, sunny and benign one minute can become a raging torrent of water with strong winds and cloudy changeable skies a few hours later. It is therefore essential to look at your chosen spot objectively to decide firstly if it is generally suited to kiteboarding, and secondly if it is suitable at that precise time.

When unpredictable, random occurrences crop up you need some knowledge of what to do and how to do it. For this reason the section on self-rescues could be your most useful read in the whole book! I have performed self-rescues more times than I care to remember in the early days, as well as while teaching and due to wind- and kit-failures. It is an easy and quick technique and doesn't damage your kit in any way if executed properly. Practise it in a sheltered area or on a light-wind day. Think and work out your exit route and make plans for scenarios when something does go wrong. Remember, a thing breaking isn't the problem: panicking when they do is.

SITE AND RISK ASSESSMENT
Risk assessment is a commonly used term in society today and it is carried out in numerous environments in order to gauge whether an activity can be executed safely in a given surrounding. Its purpose is to identify risk, and then limit this to a perceived 'acceptable' level.

When it comes to kiteboarding others often do this for us, and at most kiteboarding spots there is a common best practice that has been culturally accepted. For instance, a popular kiteboarding beach will often have an area set aside for people to use to rig up, launch, land and ride. Not always, but most commonly, this is the best practice for a given location and is probably worth following.

You should remember, however, that even the most popular kite spots don't 'work' every day. For instance, Tarifa, on Spain's southern coastline, can boast in excess of 2,000 kites on a busy day in summertime, yet in the dead of winter there may not be a single kite in sight. A situation such as this is when 'site assessment' comes into play. Kiteboarding is the one watersport above all others for which good site assessment is crucial, and it should be taken seriously.

▶ **Beyond economic repair.**

Considering your exit routes from the water if something unplanned happens is increasingly important the more advanced you get and the more challenging the environment becomes. Don't be deceived by videos of monster waves being casually ridden by someone wearing just a pair of shorts; the back-up crew is probably just out of shot and the team is usually very well prepped.

If you always go through a mental checklist, which can take as little as a minute for a regular kiteboarder at their favoured spot, then there will be no nasty surprises. Such big advances have occurred over recent years in both the ease of use and quality of equipment that the most common cause of problems at sea these days is human error, which we can all avoid.

▲ **Getting out of the sun for a second.**

THE IMPORTANCE OF 'SHOE'

There are many ways of conducting a good site assessment, but I use the acronym SHOE, which is used for teaching and in practice by everyone from beginners to experts.

SURFACE: Is the water shallow or deep, bumpy or flat? Are there hidden obstacles under the water? Is there a current or tidal flow running? Is the bottom sandy or rocky? Do you need wetsuit shoes? Are there waves, rips or nasty local effects you should know about on the beach? On land, is it sand, grass or a harder surface? Is it smooth or rough, soft or hard? Sometimes soft wet grass can be like an ice rink and pose a risk.

HAZARDS: Every beach will have physical objects on it, ranging from rocks and trees to signs, fences, buildings, cliffs and many other things. Are these hazards avoidable or is it inevitable that you will come into contact with one at some point? A generally safe minimum distance to maintain from any fixed hazard is twice the length of your kite lines, as this distance means that your kite can safely crash and be recovered before it hits anything.

OTHERS: Popular kiteboarding spots may attract lots of people wanting to participate in not only kiteboarding but also windsurfing, surfing, swimming and stand up paddle boarding (SUP). All of these people need to integrate safely and positively with each other. Sometimes a beach can simply be too crowded for safe kiteboarding to occur, so use your common sense to decide where this limit is.

ENVIRONMENT: Kiteboarders need wind, but there is such a thing as too much wind – anything over 25 knots of wind speed is best left to advanced riders only. At lower wind speeds you need to decide what your personal limit is, depending on your level, location and equipment. IF IN DOUBT DON'T GO OUT. Temperature is also a huge factor in the viability of a session. Coming from a 'fresher' part of the planet I am no stranger to cold winds and waters, but I always take precautions such as wearing a good wetsuit and warm kit. I also take more care over how far out I go and triple-check my gear before going. The cold can escalate a small issue into a serious one very quickly.

▲ The escaping bladder end can easily burst.

EQUIPMENT FAILURE

This is everyone's nightmare and sometimes cannot be helped. I remember stepping on a pal's windsurfer years ago. He was a solid 140kg (22 stone) and, at less than 70kg (11 stone), I didn't expect to snap the mast before I'd sailed 10m (33ft)! I still felt the need to reimburse him, even if it was about to go anyway and just an unfortunate time to take over. Most equipment failure, however, is preventable, or at least predictable. A severely frayed line, worn trimstrap or threaded footstrap etc will visually indicate if that piece of kit has reached the end of its life. Good kit checks should therefore be carried out regularly. You should also take care of your equipment both for safety and to prolong its life. Simple, quick things such as rinsing a bar between uses can considerably prolong its life.

SAFETY PACK-DOWN

Kiteboarding is unique in its equipment and rescue methods, since there is lots of line and the main 'engine' is a distance away from the pilot. The buoyancy of the board is also often negligible. However, packing up in the water is easy if executed correctly and is a very effective way of getting back to shore either under the pilot's own steam, by using the canopy as a sail, or by enabling a safe and complete pick-up of the pilot and kit without incurring any harm or damage to either.

Both sailing yourself home and completely packing up the kite start with the same procedure. First, you must depower the kite completely and pack up the lines to get to the kite. Make sure you know how your safety system works and what to do before you have to try it out for real on the water.

1. Release the chickenloop safety release and wrap the single safety line on to the bar, ensuring the kite is completely depowered.

2. Wrap the rest of the lines on to the bar, ensuring that the safety line is bearing the tension and the rest are not tensioned. This is often a bit messy but stick with it, and wrap the lines all the way until your reach the kite. Once you have taken hold of the kite, lock off the lines.

3. The kite will most likely be face down in the secure position on the water. There is a really easy technique to turn it over from here that involves minimal effort. Put the arm closest to the wing tip on top of the kite and hold it down, while putting your other arm and shoulder underneath and pushing up. Once air has got underneath the kite it will flip over effortlessly.

SAILING IN

If there is wind and the beach is either down or across the wind then using the kite as a sail is a brilliantly effective way of getting back to shore, and is far easier than swimming.

Once the kite is upturned with the wing tips pointing up, swim it round so the leading edge is pointing across and downwind in the desired direction of travel.

Find the top front line and, while lying on the leading-edge wing tip of the bottom side, pull in the front top line to create some tension in the canopy. Once you are moving, and have wind in your 'sail', you can adjust your position for comfort. You won't go fast but you will be able to move quicker than you would swimming and achieve an angle across the wind.

▼ **Self-rescue by sailing in steadily and safely.**

DEEP-WATER PACK-DOWN

If the wind is offshore, or has dropped, you may need to be picked up by a rescue boat. First, wait for them to signal they have seen you and are coming for you. Now you need to simply pack your kit up so the lines don't interfere with the boat and nothing gets damaged.

1. Go to the 'dump' valve on the kite and release this to deflate the leading edge (be sure the struts are locked off on a 'one-pump' system).

2. Wrap the kite from the wing tip to the centre as tidily and quickly as you can to prevent water coming in.

If the dump valve is on the wing tip then continue wrapping it all the way to the end. Now pull the other wing tip towards you while the wrapped-up side is under your arms, then reverse-roll it.

3. As soon as you have the kite completely wrapped up with the lines inside, replace the dump valve and use either your kite leash or harness to secure it all into a tidy package.

When being picked up by a rescue boat always pass them the leading edge first so the water can drain out of the kite and prevent any damage as it gets taken aboard.

▼ **Full deep-water pack-down.**

PACKING UP IN EMERGENCIES

Emergency situations are slightly different and sometimes require the breaking of some of our standard safety rules. For instance, if you have a nasty injury or are drifting on to rocks before you can salvage your equipment then you may have to release it. I always take the view that kit is replaceable but we are not, so it makes sense to look after yourself first. Be aware, however, that an abandoned kite can pose a grave danger to people downwind of you and will raise a coastguard search if you don't retrieve it and inform the authorities.

MAINTENANCE AND REPAIRS

Usually I personally don't enjoy tinkering with kit and usually end up as the 'holder' in any DIY or mechanical situation. I am the first to admit this and have built up a solid circle of kiteboarding tradesmen friends around me over the years to combat this character trait. However, despite this, I can and do frequently fix kites with ease and a little bit of enjoyment.

Kiteboarding kit is almost completely maintenance-free – a quick rinse of your bar and keeping your kit dry in the bag is normally about all that's required to keep it functioning well. Sometimes, however, some sharp grass or thorns could puncture a tube, or a carelessly placed board fin can tear the canopy. Fortunately these are both quick and easy to fix with bladder-repair patches, or glue and canopy adhesive-patches, both of which are often supplied as part of the package with your kite.

REPAIRING A KITE TUBE

This is the same as repairing a puncture in the inner tube of a bike's wheel. First you must locate the leak, which involves removing the bladder from the tube. When you do this, attach a kite-line to the end of the bladder so that the line is pulled into the tube as you remove the bladder. This allows you to pull the bladder back into the tube easily afterwards. Struts are far easier than the leading edge to remove, although the latter just requires a bit more time and effort.

Once the tube is out, a leak can sometimes be seen or felt on a cheek when the tube is inflated, but the easiest way to find it is to submerge the tube in water in order to spot the bubbles coming through the tear. A calm, warm Brazilian swimming pool is ideal for this, although a bucket of cold water will just about suffice. Once you find the leak, you can patch it with one or more adhesive patches and test it before reinserting the bladder. The adhesive patches are very effective and simple to apply. Punctures of more than about 10cm (4in) in width may require some expert patching or you may even need a replacement bladder.

REPAIRING A CANOPY TEAR

Canopy tears and small rips up to around 20cm (8in) in length can also be repaired on location very easily. Adhesive canopy cloth is available in strips and small squares. I always size this up to the offending area to fit it, then cut two identical pieces, one for each side of the canopy. I also round all the corners off in order to discourage these from rising once in contact with water.

Whether fixing a bladder or canopy, try to make the area dry, clean and out of the wind to ensure you do a good job and as little sand as possible gets on the damaged area. It is well worth carrying around a selection of bladder and canopy patches so you can fix things on the spot and not miss out on a kiteboarding session.

REPAIRING A BOARD

Boards are less commonly damaged but still require some TLC at times. Often the damage occurs while the board is in transit from home to holiday, or at the beach. Small nose dings and puncture holes in the surface are relatively easy to fix. A ding-repair kit containing fibreglass patches, resin sandpaper and a spatula, weighs hardly anything and can prevent your board taking on water or costly local repairs. I always take a roll of duct tape and surfboard wax with me on any trip too as these can also plug a temporary hole while on location.

1 **Inflate tube to find leak.**

2 **Search for bubbles.**

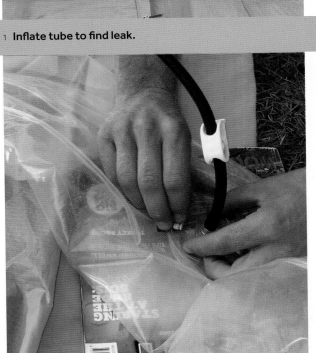

3 **Patch the hole.**

4 **Check it holds pressure.**

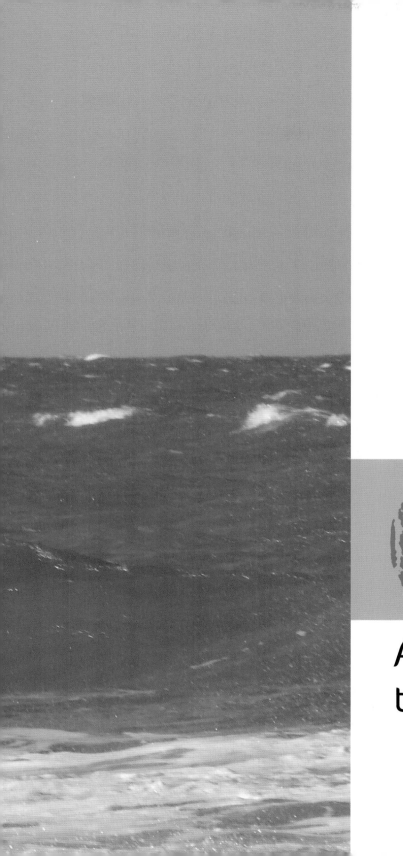

Advanced techniques

Advanced techniques

As you progress you will crave more wind, different equipment, bigger surf, flatter water and so on. It is fantastically rewarding to reach and exceed milestones in a sport. As you progress it is beneficial to increase your theoretical knowledge alongside your practical prowess, since a solid understanding of why and how something happens makes it far more likely that you will be successful when you actually come to do it. With this in mind let's clarify some sailing rules and parameters, which determine where we can and can't go when kiteboarding.

SELF-LAUNCHING AND LANDING

While self-launching is not a beginner's skill, it is extremely useful for intermediates to perform in the right area. Some beaches, such as those with confined and tricky launching areas, are completely unsuitable for self-launching. Other beaches are spacious with plenty of large, soft sandy areas, and these are perfectly safe for self-launching and indeed landing. Be aware, however, that the latter should only be attempted in light to moderate winds and you need a large amount of downwind space to be clear of any obstacles for it to be a safe, viable option.

SELF-LAUNCHING A HYBRID AND C-KITE

PREPARATION The key to every good launch is a sensible plan and solid preparation. There is nothing worse than getting halfway back to your board only to discover that you have not put enough sand on the kite's wing tip and then have to watch it self-launch

and the bar fly past you as it wings its way down the beach towards the rocks. To avoid this, you need to be careful about the amount of sand you use and where you weigh down the kite.

First of all pick your spot, making sure there's plenty of downwind run-off and that the kite is on the waterside. Fold over the lower wing tip, putting lots of the sand on the top-skin side of the folded canopy next to the leading edge. Make sure no sand goes on the inside/ bottom of the canopy as this can cause problems.

When you position the kite ensure your lines are running downwind from the kite and that the kite is flapping with more topside against the breeze than bottom-side. Once secured, take the lines and run them out to about 3m (10ft) in front of the kite, then dig them into the sand. Make sure the lines are not caught on the wing tips or the back of the canopy, so they all tension correctly.

THE LAUNCH Once you have prepared the kite, stay by it for a few seconds and look to see if it's settled and not too keen to shed the sand and bolt while you're making your way to the bar... If in doubt, use more sand. Once you decide to walk away, don't hesitate. Go straight to the bar and connect your leash before picking it up.

Walk around to a beam of the kite with a little slack in the lines. Once you're at the right angle, reverse away from the kite with an even bar, as this will tension the canopy and unfold the bottom wing tip thus removing the sand and, hey presto, the kite is launched and ready to go.

KEY POINTS:

- Put lots of sand in the right place.
- Feed the lines into the sand 3–4.5m (10–15ft) away from the canopy and bury them in the sand, ensuring they are not tangled.
- Don't hesitate and give the kite a couple of metres of power to ensure some immediate steerage once it becomes airborne.

▼ Slowly raise the kite up the side of the window, so that it stands onto its wing tip across the wind from you.

SELF-LAUNCHING A BOW KITE

Once rigged, check and attach your chickenloop and safety leash before moving from the downwind position (see page 164 for more information about chickenloop). Once attached, move up to a spot across the wind and slowly tension the lines so the kite slides around and begins to move downwind. Pull and feather the top line to raise the top wing tip.

Once the kite rises, be sure to depower to avoid being dragged forwards. Continue to the water as normal once the kite is in the air and flying in control.

SELF-LANDING

To begin with, both self-launching and self-landing are easier to perform with bridled kites than dedicated C-kites. Landing takes a bit of planning, as you need to select the right landing area, where there is plenty of space and no obstacles downwind. You must also be prepared to release the kite on to the safety leash at any point if the kite refuses to settle on the ground.

Come in slowly and get the kite settled at 3 or 9 o'clock. From here, detach the chickenloop and walk downwind and towards the kite to de-tension the lines, and at the same time give the middle top line a tug to pull down the canopy so the wind flows over the top of the kite. This will push the kite straight down into the safety position. Proceed straight to the kite and secure it, keeping hold of the leash line only, just in case it takes off during this time.

You really need to have had some expert guidance and be in the right conditions in order to practise these solo techniques safely. Seek out a good instructor at a recognised school to give you a lesson before attempting these techniques alone.

1 Remove sand and security weight.

2 Attach bar and safety leash before tensioning lines.

3 Walk to the edge of the wind window.

4 Tension the lines.

5 Let the kite roll onto the wing tip.

6 Launch slowly up the side of the neutral zone as normal.

DUAL LAUNCHING AND LANDING

Similar to solo launching and landing, a dual launch is an intermediate manoeuvre and requires both a suitable location and an adequate level of skill. If done well it is a very smooth, quick and useful procedure that allows two people to launch and land safely in an area where there are no launching assistants and solo launching is not suitable.

On occasion you and a friend might find yourself in a remote spot with no fellow-kiters around, where conditions are perfect and you are both keen to get on the water. Rather than just taking turns and having to watch each other, you could use a very effective method to double-launch and get both of you up and kiting at the same time. I tend to do this regularly on downwinders. When you are an instructor or leader there is a responsibility to get everyone launched and out before sorting out your own launch. In these situations I usually opt for launching my own kite as normal with the aid of an assistant, then launching the final student's kite while simultaneously flying my own. This multitasking aspect of dual-launching is the most difficult thing about something that is otherwise very straightforward if the wind and location are good.

In order to dual-launch successfully it is important to give yourself plenty of space and run-off. Make sure you get yourself comfortable and your own kite correctly powered and do not rush to pick up the launching kite. The best scenario is one in which you get the final pilot to hand you their kite on the opposing side to your own in the launching position, and for them to visually check the lines are not tangled for you. The safest and most logical order is to fly your own kite on the seaward side of the window fairly high, then hold the launching kite in the other hand on the landside. This way both you and the launching kite are facing the sea while launching, which makes it easier for the second pilot to align themselves quickly as they can view your kite's flying angle easily and mirror this with their own. Once you have the second kite in your hands, the

second pilot must get connected and leashed properly from a downwind position and then walk across and upwind in the same way they would for a self-launch. The key here is to tension the kite gradually rather than suddenly and to be sheeted out and correctly trimmed so as not to knock you off balance. If your kite is to starboard and being held with your right hand, the bar should be gripped on the left-central side to prevent it from falling. An outstretched left arm should hold the kite centrally between the inflation valves in the standard launch position.

KEY POINTS:

- Ensure you have enough space.
- Prepare and work out your wind angles before anything is launched.
- Get comfortable with your own kite first.
- Ask the second pilot to pass you their kite before connecting him or herself.
- Ensure the second person positions themselves gradually and communications are clear.
- Don't hang around: get it in position and get the kite launched. Then head into the water as fast as you can.

Remember these methods are verging on being intermediate to advanced techniques that require a high level of flying ability and confidence, along with a properly planned briefing in order to achieve a successful outcome. Have a plan of what to do in case of a mishap and don't hesitate to pull your release if things start going wrong.

► **Dual launching.**

THE BEACH-START

Beach- and jump-starts into super-flat water are not only cool to do and watch, but also fun and easy to learn. The flat-water lagoon jump-start is perhaps a little theoretical, as not everyone will have a freshwater mirror-flat lagoon at the end of the road, but looking at that technique will prepare you for the moment when there is.

More realistically, you are likely to encounter at least a bit of wavy shore-break and little waves on to a shelving beach. There are a number of ways to deal with this very dynamic and constantly changing environment. Often the speed and drift of the sea is not fully appreciated within this 'impact zone', where the water is not only moving towards the beach in the shape of waves, but also along it (usually downwind) and then sucking back out to sea between the waves. This side-shore drift has a nasty habit of taking all the wind out of your kite as soon as you sit down to put on your board. Fortunately it is still possible to enter the water, hop on your board and whiz

▲ **Contemplating the longest wave, Pacasmayo, Peru.**

out over this entire bumpy zone effortlessly with a bit of preparation, planning and technique.

SETTING IT UP

As I always say when teaching all the watersports I have instructed over the years, success is all in the preparation. Getting the kite in the right place, high up on the seaward side, and nicely powered with the bar about halfway down the trim is all-important. You then need to hold the board by the windward rail in front of the strap position with your front hand. There is then no rush – in fact the opposite applies – and you can stand and watch the break for a few minutes. Study how far the water surges and retracts. Timing is everything as the water can change from a surging inwards torrent to a moment of stable standing water to a dredging power-killing retraction seaward in ten seconds. The moment you choose to launch is critical to your success and getting out wipeout-free.

THE GO

In terms of timing, you want to be heading steadily into the water as a wave is surging up the beach, and you need to be off and making way before this surge becomes a backwash. This means there can be no hesitation once you have chosen your moment.

Project the board forwards across and slightly upwind of yourself. The 'lighter' you can make yourself as you step on the board the better, and you can use the kite's lift to help you here. Step on with the front foot first as this is the important one, then follow with the back foot. The front foot needs to be over the footstrap position (which is why it's far easier to do this without any straps on the board) along the centreline. As you step on you need to dive the kite to produce a bit of power and bear off very broad to get some momentum up quickly. The lighter you are on the back foot through this the better. Practising this beach start will lead to a couple of harmless wipeouts and a few mouthfuls of seawater, but once you master the technique it is an extremely useful and graceful way to get off a beach anywhere in the world.

1 Stand and place front foot into the strap, then steer the kite in the direction you want to travel.

2 As you feel the power come on, hop onto the board and don't worry too much about getting the back foot into the strap. Having your foot next to the strap is fine for the first few metres.

3 Once riding off, you can slide your back foot into the straps if it missed as you hopped on.

▲ Carving turn.

COMING IN WITH STYLE

Having finished your session there is an equally elegant and controlled technique for coming in solo. The first time you approach the beach it is best to simply slow down, sink into the board-start position and kick your board off if it has footstraps, or just let it float away to leeward if not. Stand up and walk up the remainder of the beach. Never worry about the board until the kite is landed and secured, as the board will always just wash up the beach slightly downwind, unless there is a very rare bizarre current.

This method is great for a while, but you may then watch videos and see kiteboarding heroes using dynamic and indeed drier ways to exit the water than sitting in it and walking out. With twin-tips the ultimate exit is to cruise in towards the beach with power in the kite, then go into a jump-transition on the shoreline, making sure not to impede others and that there is sufficient space. Once floating in the air for a second, reach down, remove the board and land softly on both feet with your board in your hand, then calmly walk up the beach and land the kite.

This of course takes practice and a prerequisite ability of being able to jump-transition competently. Once mastered it is not only useful to avoid dumping shore-break, but wins ultimate 'cool points'. As with mastering beach starts, be prepared to take a few face-plants and possibly embarrass yourself a little during this entertaining learning process. I know I certainly did. It is advisable to choose a spacious uncrowded area of beach with softer sand to perfect this technique.

On directional boards without straps the technique is different but has the same end result, and kudos or embarrassment, depending on the level of success.

SETTING IT UP

Prepare and plan properly, looking at where you are going to come in, how fast, and what the shore-break and beach surface is like. The timing and the speed of approach are very important. Needless to say, pick a quiet spot, free from crowds or any hazards on the shoreline or beach.

▼ **Coming in solo.**

1 Slow your speed, raise your kite with tension and prepare to dismount.

2 As you descend the board, it should pop up as your weight is released.

3 Connect your palm with the windward rail to push this down and make the board go vertical rail to rail. At this point it will sit under your arm beautifully, hopefully.

4 Walk out smiling.

Come in and scope the area once, gauging the water's depth and movement and the kite's power first. For this move, unlike downhill skiing, speed is not your friend. You need to shed all the speed you can, flying the kite high in the window, still in the direction of travel so you have planing momentum, but slowly with lots of lift in the kite, as this will help you to stand.

THE GO

Bear away slightly, slowing more as you do so, then carve to windward very slightly.

Press/load the board quickly but lightly, then gently hop off to leeward (downwind) of the board, with your back foot first.

The front foot needs to flick the windward rail downwards as the board pops up so the wind blows this rail down and seamlessly blows the whole thing sideways on to your side and under your arm.

KEY POINTS:

- Slow down.
- Bear off, then carve to wind and gently pop.
- Hop off, pushing the windward rail down.
- The board will automatically travel downwind on to your side, so have your arm up to grab it into your armpit.

It is important that the water depth is correct: it should be about knee- to thigh-high. If it is too shallow you could twist your ankle, and if it is too deep you may find yourself in an interesting body-drag with a board somewhere under your armpit!

KITING WITH BOAT SUPPORT

Although perfectly safe, when accidents occur in kiteboarding they generally result from the pilot losing control of the kite for a variety of reasons and colliding with something solid on the shore. If you remove the shoreline and its associated obstacles by getting some water wheels and learning in deeper open expanses of water, you not only reduce the collision factor greatly, but you can also avoid the walk of shame.

Kiteboarding from a boat is safe and greatly expands both your access to kiteable locations and wind-direction options. It does, however, require a certain degree of logistics and preparation in order to get launched and packed up again tidily. Remembering a pump, for instance, is a must if you are going far from land, as borrowing the guy next door's one is not really an option. There is also a very simple but specific way to rig your kite to allow it to be erected off the side of the boat with the lines correctly attached. This has to be done in advance and the kite needs to be stowed carefully to ensure success.

All the standard logistics of taking a boat to sea will of course also apply and need to be considered, including crew, fuel, weather and the craft's suitability; just because someone has a fishing boat does not mean it will lend itself to being a good kiteboard-launching platform. The methods used for rigging, launching, relaunching, coaching and safety cover when using a boat can all be learned with a local school that teaches in these environments.

The advantages of kiteboarding from a boat are primarily an increase in space and the ability to cover distance, whether you are learning to ride upwind or kiting downwind along a coastline or across a lake or channel, and travelling back safely. Racing benefits from being done in uncrowded and deep areas of open water, which can be found and utilised far more effectively with a boat present both as a support and a means of transportation.

Despite the unavoidable fact that access to many boats remains beyond the reach of most people's budgets, there is no denying that large private yachts can provide a fantastic platform from which to kiteboard at some unique and secluded spots, while avoiding the crowds on the beach and obstacles in the water. However, even if you intend to use a boat frequently and avoid going ashore, it is still worth learning to rig and launch from a beach environment as this is by far the most common entry location, and these essential skills need to be grasped at an early stage when learning to kiteboard.

I have been lucky enough to teach on a few floating hotels and, while their opulence is second-to-none, they are not very manoeuvrable when it comes to launching and collecting you from the water, which is why in reality you often find yourself launching and coaching from the ribs or jet skis. If the crew will allow it, it's possible to rig on the deck and let your kite drift off the back to launch and start with style. Just be careful of your own wind shadow and the cleats.

▼ **This sequence shows a full deep-water pack-down being carried out.**

09

Points of sailing

Points of sailing

As well as being a free-spirited sport full of extreme stunts, kiteboarding is a sailing discipline. As such, the basic rules of sailing apply for travelling across, towards and away from the wind. There is, however, an incredibly exciting and somewhat complex third dimension to kiteboarding that allows the rider unprecedented amounts of airtime and record-breaking speeds downwind.

The directions you can travel in on any sailing craft are: across the wind (a 'beam reach'); across and downwind (a 'broad reach'); dead downwind (a 'dead run'); and towards the wind ('close-hauled').

BEAM REACH

The basic goal of all sail sports is to travel across the wind at 90 degrees (a beam reach), turn around and return to the same spot. Kiteboarding is no different and once you master this beam reach, the world is your oyster. A lot of time is initially spent walking back to your start point (the walk of shame), and it's a great day when you stop having to do this. The term 'beam' means the side of a boat.

BROAD REACH

This is the fastest point of sailing and is the most exciting. As you gain speed the forces of apparent wind demand that your course gradually becomes more and more broad to the wind. The optimum angle off the wind depends on the craft, the wind speed and the resistance of the hull. For instance, snowkiters or icekiters can experience far less resistance over the surface and therefore can achieve broader and greater speeds. On a broad reach it is possible to travel faster than the true wind speed. In fact this is common for windsurfers and kiteboarders, which makes this point all the more exhilarating.

DEAD RUN

A dead run occurs when you are travelling in the same direction as the true wind, and for every sailing discipline – except kiteboarding – the maximum speed is that gained at true wind speed minus whatever drag the craft creates. While sailing races such as the America's Cup and SailGP, as well as events for all manner of hydrofoiling craft, are getting ever closer and faster downwind, these vessels are still forced on to very broad reaches to allow apparent wind resistance to exceed the wind's true speed.

Kiteboarding, however, allows you to throw your engine around the sky across the power zone of the wind window, and create more power by harnessing the kite's motion. This is completely unique to kiteboarding and gives the sport a fundamental advantage in racing around a course, along with exhilarating downwind potential. Its

▲ **The author at work with windsurfer pal in Brazil.**

inclusion in the Paris Olympics will serve to demonstrate these blistering speeds as athletes continue to exceed speeds of three times the gradient windspeed on marginal wind days.

CLOSE-HAULED/CLOSE REACH

Moving towards the wind at an angle greater than 90 degrees is possible for all sailing craft. How much this angle can be reduced, so that the vessel is sailing close-hauled at the most acute angle possible, is determined by their design. An intermediate kiteboarder with a regular twin-tip and reasonable technique can expect to achieve an angle of around 70–45 degrees towards the true wind. Kitefoil boards, such as those used on the IKA World Cup series, are now achieving incredible angles, for example in excess of 60 degrees to windward, by using high performance foils, lightweight and efficient Ram Air kites and expert technique.

APPARENT WIND

Once you start moving under any sail power the wind window changes, and another important element, called apparent wind, comes into play. This is the wind experienced by a moving object. On a windless day the apparent wind is equal to the velocity of the moving object, so if you were to cycle at a velocity of 20kph (12.5mph) then the apparent wind would also be 20kph. If there were a 'true wind' of, say 5kph (3mph), coming from due north of the direction you were cycling in (a headwind) then this would be added to the velocity of the moving object: 20kph + 5kph = 25mph of apparent wind. If there were a true wind of 5kph coming from due south of the direction you were travelling in (a tailwind) then this would be deducted from the velocity of the moving object: 20kph – 5kph = 15kph of apparent wind.

These calculations are based on the motion of the bike being parallel to the true wind, but when the motion is not parallel to the true wind then trigonometry is required in order to calculate the apparent wind (see below, the apparent wind equation).

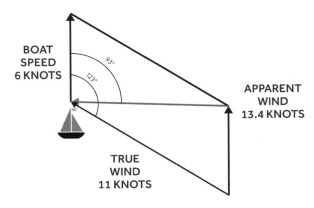

>>> **The apparent wind equation.**

▼ **This diagram shows apparent wind, the wind experienced by a moving object.**

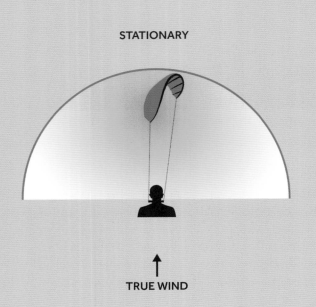

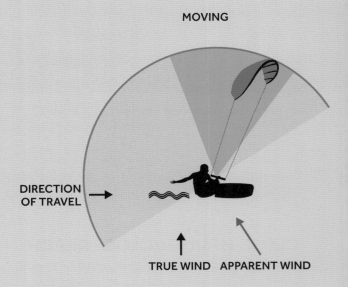

For instance, if you were to cycle the same route but there was now an onshore wind at 90 degrees to your direction of travel, the apparent wind you would feel would come from 45 degrees in front and 45 degrees to the side.

When sailing on any type of moving craft, if either the speed of the true wind or the velocity of the craft is increased beyond the other's, the angle of the apparent wind would change a corresponding amount. If both the true wind and the velocity are equal or increase equally, the apparent wind will continue to come at a 45-degree angle. In reality, these two elements are changing constantly.

In sailing disciplines such as ice-yachting or ice-kiting the surface friction is very small, which allows the sailor to increase the craft's velocity far in excess of the speed of the true wind. As a result, skilled pilots on these craft can zoom around at incredible angles to the true wind, and there are elaborate courses similar to go-cart tracks on frozen Scandinavian lakes, which make use of this potential and the relative insignificance of the true wind's direction. Pilots of ice-yachts are able to push the craft to gain initial speed then, through skilful helming and trimming of their sails, race the course on their own apparent wind.

As a kiteboarder, it is useful to have an understanding of the effect of apparent wind and then to use it to your advantage. As we see in the next section on riding upwind, it is not the fastest kiter who can get upwind the most efficiently, but the one with the best speed and velocity made good (VMG) or upwind angle once planing. Of course when you enter the racing world, factors such as speed and pointing angles – along with local wind-effect knowledge, good equipment, a little bit of luck … and not falling off! – become the difference between gold and silver medals. However, as a beginner, intermediate, or even advanced kiteboarder you don't really need to worry about the technical equations and numerical angles of potential efficiency within apparent wind, since the variables of the tide, your equipment, the water state, and what you might be wearing at the time, can all throw these calculations right out of the window. If you are racing towards the Olympics then pick up a maths book! For us mere mortals, I would recommend you get your head around managing your speed and edging the board, and then experiment with pointing up- and downwind as far as you can to feel the effect of apparent wind for yourself. This will physically show you not only the limits in each direction, but also what you have to do with the kite to achieve the optimum speed, and what happens when you get the angle wrong.

Foiling is generally pressure testing a lot of the rules, angles and speeds sailors can travel, and kiters are arguably doing this the most. The ability to travel faster than the breeze dead downwind does pose a few new and unique rules, and in these exceptional instances it all comes down to moving your kite without crashing, and being able to maintain speed and control, of which I am still enjoying the challenge!

MOVING FASTER

DIRECTION OF TRAVEL

APPARENT WIND

TRUE WIND

Going upwind

10

Going upwind

No kiteboarder can deny that they have done the walk of shame at least once, if not a hundred times, during their kiteboarding career. On certain days even the best pros in the business have to trudge the shoreline, remembering the early days. But how can we reduce this to a minimum, and simply sail back to where we started?

With the right kit, in the right place and with the right wind it's possible for everyone to be able to hold their ground and return to the spot they started out from. This is the Holy Grail, the light, the key, independent kiteboarding – whatever you describe it as – the ability to travel upwind opens up a whole new world for your kiteboarding and allows you to go out and come back to the same point. The key to riding upwind is the successful interaction of the kite, the board and the pilot.

In recent years, the rise of the foil has made upwind performance very different. Sometimes, when foiling, the walk of shame back down the beach is in the early days. The foil is in its element heeled over driving to windward and this is arguably the most secure position for it. Standing the mast vertical and riding off the wind, literally balancing on the sword, is somewhat trickier.

However, prior to jumping on one of these incredible upwind machines, one must first master getting upwind on a standard planning hull. This is where some basic ground rules and techniques come in.

THE KITE

When learning how to go upwind, make sure you have an appropriate-sized kite for the conditions and the rider. Trimming the kite correctly to ensure the angle of attack is suitable (see the 'Angle of attack' section on page 25) is the first place to start, and this can be done on the beach to ensure the kite is not over-sheeted or generating too much drag. If the angle of attack is either too great or too small it will hinder your progress significantly. Any flaring of the wing tips is a sign that there's too much rear-line tension. Slackness in the rear lines means there's too much front-line tension. The 'balance/correct trim point' is different on every kite, so the best way to tell is by feel. If it responds and feels and looks good, it's probably about right. Often I apply a bit more trim when sailing towards the wind to decrease the canopy angle to the breeze, which allows the kite to fly further forward in the window.

THE BOARD

Making sure you have the right-sized board or even choosing a slightly bigger board when learning how to ride upwind will make the process far easier. Using a

board with a greater surface area, a shallower rocker line (the curve of the board) and a sharper rail in combination with big fins will result in greatly improved upwind performance.

THE RIDER

Successful upwind riding depends on the rider's stance. Imagine your body like a link in the chain between your engine (the kite) and your wheels (the board). The better this link transfers the power from one to the other, the more efficient and further upwind you will travel.

Once you have mastered this, as I have alluded to, jumping on a foil can enhance upwind performance dramatically. This in turn increases the ability to maintain ground and enjoy lighter wind sessions. The minimum windspeed on the kite foil racing tour is 5 knots average. It's impossible to maintain ground to windward on standard equipment, but foiling enables very effective course racing. It also brings extreme enjoyment in light and moderate breezes to the average Joe or Jane at the local beach as it is quite straightforward to blast around on an intermediate foil and an intermediate level in 10–12 knots, which was previously a real challenge.

► **Kitesurfing heaven in Patos, Brazil.**

THE BASIC POINTS OF STANCE:

- Your head should be facing and focussed on where you want to go, since where your head goes your body follows.
- Your shoulders should be the furthest part of your body to windward.
- Your back should be reasonably straight and your hips should be pushed forwards and upright, allowing the chest to be puffed out and twisted forwards. Keep your hips and shoulders back and try to make a straight line from your head to your front foot.
- Your front leg should be reasonably straight and applying good amounts of heel pressure on to the windward rail to effect positive edging with the front foot, curling it up. Twist your shoulders to face forwards.
- Your back leg needs to be bent, allowing the rail to be engaged and the front leg to direct the board.

▼ Bad stance.

▼ Good stance.

▲ The walk of shame.

FAQ

Why am I going fast but not upwind?
Going too fast is probably the most common reason for you not being able to travel upwind efficiently. Excess speed can be caused by lots of things: too big a kite, the wind being too strong, the board being too big or over-finned, bad edging technique or incorrect stance.

Why is the optimum upwind speed a slow, controlled planing one?
The reason for this is the faster you travel, the greater the effect apparent wind has over you. As the apparent wind moves further in front of you it prevents you from pointing upwind as far – in fact it forces you on to a broad reach, hence why this is the fastest point of sailing. Good advice for going upwind is to get planing, control this speed and then perfect your stance and edging efficiency.

Why do I keep stopping when I'm going upwind?
Edging too hard, which forces the kite forwards in the wind window, results in slowing and ultimately stopping. Once you are riding with power and momentum more edge pressure can be applied. If this is done excessively and too early, however, it is like putting on the handbrake.

Why do I travel upwind better in one direction?
This is quite common for two reasons. First, everyone always tends to be better in one direction than the other initially. Often this is travelling to the right on a starboard tack (or riding 'regular'). As your technique improves your ability will even out so that you can travel easily on both tacks. The second reason is that one direction has a better wind angle or cleaner wind. In racing terms this is known as you 'gaining tack'. This effect can be caused by the topography of the land and local wind effects. In racing, gaining tack can be the difference between winning or finishing mid-fleet if you get it right.

RIDING TOESIDE

So you are riding up and down, turning with a dry bum and holding your line to windward. Good work, you are doing well. It's time to start showing off.

Riding toeside is arguably the first 'freestyle' move you can do. For no particular reason, other than showing off your prowess and hoping for applause, it is possible to slide the board around so your toes are pointing into the wind and water and, with a twisted body and nonchalant one-handed grip, you can continue to cruise along in the same direction as the new coolest cat on the block. It's an easy skill to practise and master and once you have it in the bag you can start using it to impress your friends and add some pizzazz to your kiteboarding straight away. Riding toeside also opens the freestyle door to a host of tricks since it increases your control and directional stability, and it saves a bit of back-leg burn on longer tacks too.

Practising 'switching' to toeside is easy and very low-impact in terms of wipeouts and consequence, as the most common thing to happen when learning the skill is a rather gradual sinking feeling as you head towards the kite and squeeze the life from your control bar. The best direction to practise in is opposite your dominant or favoured tack: for instance a regular rider who prefers riding with the left leg leading should ride to the right with their right leg forwards the first time they try toeside, since this enables you to switch to your preferred direction of left leg leading.

When sliding from your heel to toe edge, there is no reason for the kite to be affected and you should aim to continue in the same direction at the same speed. Keep the kite fairly high in the intermediate zone and in the direction of travel. Plan and prepare your spot so you don't end up riding for a kilometre 'thinking' about the move rather than actually doing it!

▲ **Riding normally.**

▲ **Sliding board around.**

The first thing to do is get going at a comfortable and controllable speed. Drop your front hand from the bar and let it hang to windward, as this allows your shoulders to open and your body to twist more easily.

Push your back leg downwind and around to face the direction of travel at the same time as twisting your hips and leaning your chest and torso windward.

This whole movement takes a second and, once your hand comes off, should involve smooth standing up and sliding round of the board.

Once you are on to your toeside, lean your body weight through the harness to give you some toeside edge-pressure. Keeping your arm off the bar will really help you do this. Be aware that you won't be able to edge as hard on your toes as you can on your heels, so try not to go too fast.

A common error at this stage is to focus on the kite rather than the direction of travel once you are on your toes. The phrase 'where your head goes, your body follows' could not be more true here and looking at the kite will lead to you following it, which results in a lack of edge pressure that will depower the kite and cause you to come to a slow and reluctant sinking halt. To combat this, try to continue in exactly the same direction as before you switched. Picking something out on the horizon or in front of you will help with this.

KEY POINTS:

- Plan and check your spot, and stick to it.
- Keep the kite cruising along and drop your front hand.
- Twist your hips at the same time as sliding your back leg around.
- Lean to windward through your harness.

▲ **Weight forwards.**

▲ **Riding toeside.**

TURNING AND TRANSITIONS

We have already examined the elementary method of turning around: slowing down, sitting down, water-starting in the other direction or using the sitting-gybe. Once this is mastered you move on to the training gybe, a faster turn throughout which the rider stands up. When using a twin-tip this is without doubt the most common type of turn, and unlike any other sailing discipline it does not require the moving of your feet and a carving redirection of the board, a skill that can take windsurfers a lifetime to achieve. As its name suggest, a 'twin-tip' – which is comparable to a wakeboard or snowboard – has two identical ends and one dominant windward or 'heel edge'. These make turning around infinitely easier.

Once the training gybe is in the bag, you can move on to the next manoeuvre, the heel-to-toeside carve. Working through these techniques in this order is not only logical, but it will also serve to prevent accidents and injuries, as a gradual progression will build confidence and an awareness of personal limitations too.

HEEL-TO-TOESIDE CARVE

This is where the fun really begins! Having mastered riding toeside you can now link this with the basic turning methodology and start layering on the 'mustard'. There are 101 ways to turn around both on the water and above it, but the heel-to-toeside carve is one of the easiest to learn, most useful and best-looking of these. It involves carving the board in an arc and following the kite around the corner with some speed. It is such a showy and impressive-looking skill that photos of super-pro riders in bikinis and shorts drawing a perfect arc over crystal waters will grace brochure covers for years to come.

The key to success in the carve is getting the final quarter of the turn right. Let's look at the heel-to-toeside carving turn in detail: As with riding toeside and upwind, first you must be planing comfortably and give yourself lots of space in which to practise.

To initiate the turn, raise the kite with controlled speed up through 12 o'clock and into the new tack. At the same time, bring your body forwards, releasing the windward edge, and transfer some weight on to your toes. The back foot is generally in charge here and applies pressure to the toe edge with a bent leg and leant-forward stance.

As the kite goes around the corner, simply follow it with the board while leaning forwards and carving a semi-circle in the water.

Just like riding toeside, the same common habit gets us all in the beginning. Once you are around to the point where you are heading towards the kite, don't stop carving. Keep on the toe edge, with your body weight now leaning to windward. Bend the back leg and feel free to drop your new back hand (the left one in this case).

Look for your trail in the water where you came from and try to cross over it as soon as you can in the new direction.

▼ Heel-to-toeside carve.

1 Stand upright and start to send the kite round the corner.

KEY POINTS:

- Plan your turning spot and check around you for other riders.
- Lean forwards, release the windward edge and follow the kite.
- Carve all the way around and try to retrace your line back in the new direction.

As mentioned earlier, we are all wired in one direction, regular or goofy. Goofy footers will probably find this carve easier from starboard on to port. Regulars should try the other end first.

2 Lean forwards onto your toes and into the corner.

3 Continue to lean on your toes into the turn following the kite around a smooth arc.

4 Continue carving towards your previous track. Don't follow the kite onto a broad reach at this point.

5 Ride out across the wind on your toes.

TOE-TO-HEELSIDE CARVE

Another variation on carving turns is to slide around on to your toeside edge before the turn, then carve back on to your heels. This allows you to exit the turn with confidence, and thus more speed and style, as you are back to a more stable riding position on your heel edge. It's also a great way to practise waveriding carves on the face of the wave in the future.

The manoeuvre is simply a combination of sliding the board around on to your toes – which we have looked at in the riding toeside section – then following the carving technique seen in the heel-to-toeside turn but with the edges reversed. Once you have turned on to your toeside, raise the kite up again, release the windward (toeside) edge and follow the kite around the turn.

The exit should be more comfortable, which is why you can progress this turn to be tighter, faster and more dynamic, and wow the crowd with some spray.

You'll find one of these carves, heel-to-toe or toe-to-heel, is comfortable on one tack and the other on the other tack. It is worth practising both combinations on both tacks to improve your double-sided ability and general control. It's great fun to ride upwind a few hundred metres then link these turns together while moving the kite positively from one side to the other, which is essentially what a waverider is doing on the face of a wave!

▼ **Toe-to-heelside carve.**

1 Riding on the topside, raise your body upright and begin looking into the turn.

2 Initiate the turn with the kite and follow with your weight onto your back foot and heels.

3 Twist your front shoulder into the turn and carve hard with your heels.

4 Lean into the turn and continue carving towards your previous track before the turn.

5 Ride back across your previous track in a normal heelside stance.

▼ **Jump transition**

1 Lift and stop moving forwards.

2 Crunch and hold.

JUMP TRANSITION

Another way to turn, which again is completely unique to kiteboarding, is to jump, hang gracefully in the air (as if someone has hit a pause button), then smoothly land and zoom off in the other direction. Combining this with a high-five with a pal on the beach or wave quite simply immortalises your 'coolness', (or at least it feels that way at the time).

To jump transition you basically need to perform a really aggressive training gybe with lots of upwind carving and positive kite steering. In many sports there are often a few techniques that are a little tricky to describe but which, once you have 'felt it', are completely natural. The floaty bit in the jump transition is just like this and it can also be 'felt' during tacking; when you have the kite in exactly the right position for a split second it suspends you beautifully and gives you all the time in the world to plan the next bit of the move.

3 Redirect.

4 Extend to land.

This moment occurs when you stop travelling in one direction as a result of having carved aggressively upwind, at which point you send the kite through 12 o'clock positively but gradually, which creates lift and suspends you in the air. As soon as this happens, you need to redirect the kite in the new direction, which serves to soften your landing as you begin to move on the new tack. Lots of line tension and leg bend need to be used here to aid the lift and soften the landing.

As your technique improves – and your subsequent fan club grows – you can go higher and get more stylish, doing grabs of the board, waves to the crowd and even rotation of the body. One hint my wife always gives for jump transitions is that if your abs are not on fire after practising a dozen, then you're doing it wrong.

GYBING

Known as 'jibing' in the USA, this common sailing term refers to the turning around of a unidirectional craft where the bow or front passes downwind through 180 degrees. It can be a fast and exciting turn to do on a range of craft, from kites and windsurfers to all forms of sailing.

Learning the gybe on a directional kiteboard requires some practice and determination, but is more than achievable by all intermediates. Riding a directional

comfortably is a good place to start and is very straightforward. I get people to practise this first so they can go across the wind, edge and control their speed and try riding toeside before attempting to gybe. Once you can do this, the gybe essentially comes down to switching your feet either before or after the carve.

The conventional gybe consists of riding along, steering the kite across the window and following this in a carving arc from heel-to-toeside.

Then, on exiting the arc with an upright stance, switch your feet to get your heels back on the windward edge.

Common problems mainly occur while exiting the move around the foot switch. It feels more natural to lean back and stand on the tail of the board momentarily, which is wrong. Try to lean forwards and bring the back foot up next to the front foot to switch them. It is also common to head off downwind on toeside following the kite and gradually slowing down. Practise riding across the wind comfortably on toeside to combat this. Dropping the front hand often helps to open the body to windward and edge the toeside rail more positively.

Using one particular end will always be easier and feel more natural than the other in the beginning. However, it is best to practise at both ends so you become confident using either. You can also try to switch your feet on to toeside before the carve as an alternative technique, which is easier if you are comfortable in only one toeside direction.

▼ **Gybing strap to strap.**

1 Stand upright on the board and begin to redirect the kite through 12 o'clock.

2 Lean forwards onto the front foot and topside, following the kite into the turn.

3 Continue to carve around towards the new direction of travel.

4 Keep weight on the front foot and carve past the kite, don't follow it.

5 With your weight on the front foot, bring the back foot level and switch feet on the front pad.

6 Ride out heeled as normal.

TACKING

Tacking is the opposite to gybing: it results in the same change of direction, but involves the nose of the board travelling upwind through the eye of the wind to turn. It also requires a switching of the feet and involves the board turning 180 degrees. It is regarded as the more difficult turn in kiteboarding, which is different from most other sailing disciplines. This is because kiteboarding is a planing sport, with not much displacement potential, so the timing has to be right in a kiteboarding tack or the rider will sink or capsize.

Tacking is an upwind turn and, once mastered, is incredibly useful when you need to maintain or gain ground to windward. In racing, all upwind beats are tacked up by all the racers, then gybed downwind.

The technique for tacking is to head in control upwind, carving and slowing the board's speed as the kite rises above your head.

As the kite reaches the zenith and the board begins to stop, a 'flick' of the feet pushes the nose through the wind and allows the feet to land heelside on the board in the new direction.

At the same time, the kite is dived in the new direction to produce some power in that course.

Tacking is all about timing and, when learning, it tends to go well or nowhere for a while until you feel the 'balance' point. A proficient kiteboarder makes tacking look very smooth and easy, but in reality this is the end result of a considerable chunk of practice-time, and probably many wipeouts.

▼ **Tacking.**

1 Carve upwind and slow down with high kite.

2 As you stop, steer the kite over and flick the board through the wind with your front foot.

3 Sheet in on the bar to hold you up.

4 Push the board around to across the wind on the new track.

5 Look and dive the kite where you want to go.

6 Ride out and power up the kite accordingly.

THE BOTTOM TURN AND WAVERIDING

Riding waves is a fantastic feeling and being on a kite allows you to escape all the paddling and many of the wipeouts involved with conventional surfing. The crux of the ability to ride waves lies in the entry into the wave, which comes from the 'bottom turn'. This is the carve downwind in front of the wave before you head back up towards the breaking lip or crest.

To start with, you obviously shouldn't pick huge, plunging breakers to practise on. Instead, find a small wave with a shape that is easy to surf for your first attempts. Take the heelside-to-toeside carve manoeuvre from the gybe technique and apply it on to the face of the wave, except instead of switching your feet and heading over the top of the wave back out to sea, you need to carve back on to your heels and head round into another bottom turn, making a snake-like pattern on the surface of the wave. This sounds more difficult than it is; the most challenging part is getting into the right place. Once on the wave, its energy will help propel you along, redirecting you down the wave. The kite needs to be flown positively and should always be one step ahead of the rider at any point to ensure continued momentum.

I often get people to practise linking carving turns on downwinders to get the feeling of moving the kite aggressively and going from heel- to toe-edge

comfortably. Once you have mastered the technique, you will be on a never-ending progression curve as you strive to take on ever-steeper and bigger waves.

▲ **Committed carving.**

Airtime

11

Airtime

So, why did you take up kiteboarding? Go on, admit it, it was to get some air. As a species we have an abiding affection for flying, and kiteboarding is the watersport that brings us closest to being able to do it. The icing on the cake is that kiteboarding also enables you to perform amazing tricks, spins, loops and more. Kiteboarding jumps higher, further and more aggressively than any other watersport. New records are being broken for height and amplitude regularly. The current world record for the highest jump is 34.8m, by Maarten Haeger. That's almost two cricket pitches ... or half the wingspan of a 747 aeroplane. So, how do you begin to scale these dizzy heights? Well let's start small, with unsticking the board from the water.

THE CHOP HOP

The secret to successful jumping is to build the skills gradually and safely to avoid going too high too soon. Let's start by looking at getting the board out of the water and back on to it with some style and control.

The chop hop doesn't need to affect the kite at all; it remains constant throughout the trick, which makes it the easiest type of 'air' to get first as there is less to worry about. Instead it is all to do with the tension in the lines and the edge pressure on the board.

First, you need to have some riding space and be correctly powered up and in control. Plan your spot in the same way as you would for other moves. Begin by edging to windward and bending your knees a little to increase the line-tension. Don't overdo the edging or leg bend – begin gradually and build it up.

Once you have created some extra tension, release the heel edge and 'pop' off your toes, as if you were rising on to your tiptoes on dry land. As soon as you leave the water, lean your head forwards, push the bar down and in a little and bend your legs up.

This all happens pretty quickly and before you know it you will be at the apex of the jump. At this point you need to bring your legs back down underneath you and point the board downwind towards the kite, ready to land.

Once on the water, carve on to your original direction across the wind and await the cheers and applause!

▼ The chop hop.

1 Edge hard and create some tension in the lines.

2 Pop up from the water, lean your head forward and sheet in and down with the bar.

3 Look where you want to land.

4 Hold in the air.

KEY POINTS:

- Plan your spot, prepare your kit, and ensure you have adequate speed and space in which to practise.
- Edge a little to windward, then pop on to your toes and lean forwards. Once airborne, bend your knees.
- Spot your landing, point the board downwind and bend your knees as you touch down to absorb the bumps.

5 Extend and land broad and slightly downwind.

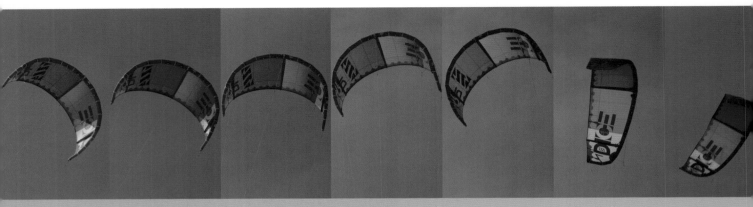

▲ **This sequence shows the kite in a pendulum-type pattern.**

SENDING THE KITE

Once you have mastered the chop hop and are popping all over the place, it is time to get the kite involved. Sending the kite in a pendulum-type pattern lifts the pilot into the air without the need for a ramp. This means, with good technique, the biggest, most impressive airs can be 'boosted' on completely flat water; yet another reason why kiteboarding is the coolest sport ever.

This pendulum motion happens in three stages and is a combination of edging and releasing the board. The more aggressive the edge and sending of the kite, the bigger the jump.

THE TAKE-OFF

The pendulum can be described as going from a high forwards position in the direction of travel, say 1 o'clock, back through 12 o'clock to 11 o'clock. This action lifts the pilot from the water.

At the same time as the kite moves it is important to edge the board progressively, then release it as the kite pulls up. The more simultaneous the occurrence of these two moves the better your take-off will be and the higher the jump. The goal here is to take off as vertically as possible. This means you reach the apex of the jump quickly, and the faster you reach the top the more time you will have on the way down.

If the timing of the kite movement and the board edging is out then the result can be varied, ranging from no lift at all to a water-skimming, uncontrolled levitation-type move that often ends with two splashes – first the pilot and then three or four seconds later the kite, because this has ended upwind of the pilot and therefore gravity prevails.

Sage advice here is to start off small and build up the take-off as you get more used to the second two parts of the jump.

AIRTIME

Once in the air, don't forget to smile! I think some of my most contorted expressions have been captured while I have been mid-air. This is a great moment and everyone remembers their best air of the day or year, often embellishing actual measurements for beer-time wow-factor too.

While in the air it is essential to maintain some body position and control to prevent being swung off balance. The easiest way to do this is to sheet in the bar so it is tensioned. This will also engage the kite better and increase the steering speed. Bend your legs up and lean forwards with your head (which feels all wrong when your body is telling you to lean back), protect the head and stick your legs out to save you.

All this time the kite needs to be above you high in the sky around 12 o'clock. Moving it forwards in the direction of travel is important, although you shouldn't move it too far; keeping it steady and high is the primary objective.

Often after a good jumping day your abs, shoulders and arms can ache a lot if you're doing it right, as they are holding your body in position and suspending it for prolonged periods of time.

THE LANDING

Every jump has a landing and, needless to say, some are better than others. The key to a good controlled landing is getting the take-off right, as you will then be able to maintain good positioning through the air time.

As you stop ascending and start descending back towards the water you need to steer the kite positively forwards so it is descending in the window in the direction you want to land in. At the same time your forwards-leaning bent-leg stance needs to open up and you need to lean forwards more with you head (honestly).

The board needs to be pointing very broad (downwind) towards the kite so that when it touches down, water is flowing from one end to the other, not from toe to heelside. As you touch down, bend your knees to absorb the landing and ensure the kite doesn't continue diving into the water.

Once you are in control, after a second or two carve back on to your beam-reach track across the wind to avoid losing too much ground downwind, or sinking as a result of following the kite too much.

A common mistake when learning to jump is leaning back and raising your legs. However alien it may feel, try to keep upright. When landing, the board should never touch down on a beam reach 90 degrees to the wind – it always need to be pointing broad. The faster the landing the broader the angle.

LOOPING THE KITE

If it is done with power and conviction, looping the kite is similar to looping a windsurfer. When a kite is looped there is a point of no return, past which you have to hold on and keep believing. This is 'the feeling' that many kiteboarders crave as it commits you to an action and requires conviction to see it through, plus it simply feels great. It has become the gauge by which the professionals are measured. Events like the Red Bull King of the Air, held in the nuclear winds of Cape Town, has demonstrated what amazing spectacles this sport can produce, with riders upwards of 20m in the air, in 40+ knots of wind, upside down, looping their kites beneath them, covering multiple hundreds of metres over the ground and landing perfectly, like a plane touching down at breakneck speeds.

The technique is fairly simple: jump into the air and pull on the back-hand end of the bar. The kite will then loop 360 degrees while travelling in an opposing direction to the rider, creating vast amounts of pull and lift. The execution, however, is far from it. The term 'megaloop' has become synonymous among the elite, who now perform multiple spins and unhooked freestyle manoeuvres, even riding strapless boards while 'megalooping'. Going big is easy for everyone to appreciate whether they kiteboard or not.

These moves are of course not for everyone, and should be attempted gradually with less power and at lower heights to begin with. The addiction to kitelooping is, however, a big draw for many people within the sport.

LOOPING YOURSELF

The forward loop in windsurfing is a formidable manoeuvre that separates windsurfers into two categories: those who can and those who can't. In kiteboarding, a forward (or more commonly backward) loop is both easier on you and the equipment. At this stage, if you are competent and able to jump and have tried the BLT jump, then a conventional backroll or loop is a straightforward next step.

The backloop can either be done without sending the kite – making it a low, reasonably fast move – or by sending the kite, which can transform it into a beautiful flowing air move.

Without sending the kite, the key is the kite's positioning, which needs to be high in the window in the direction of travel, combined with lots of backfoot lift and pressure on the take-off to create lift, and clear your head from the water as you rotate.

Ride along at a controlled speed, edge and pop positively off the back foot, then look where you want to go and bend your legs. The rest tends to happen at this point. Looking over your shoulder will make you rotate, and bending your legs speeds up rotation.

Spotting your landing is a common and almost overused phrase but it makes sense. If you are looking over your front shoulder you will see the ground or landing area early. Fix your eyes on this and your body will follow. Bending your knees as you land will absorb some impact, then continue riding.
Common problems are mainly caused by the back hand end of the bar. It is not unusual to pull on this for balance on the way round, which will send the kite in the wrong direction and cause you to crash. If you need to, let go of the back hand altogether or put it in the middle of the bar to minimise erroneous inputs.

THE FORWARD LOOP

Forward loop rotations require the sending of the kite and a bit of technique to initiate the forward rotation. They are often a slower and smoother rotation than the backloop. The sequence is shown below.

▼ Forward (front) loop with a grab.

1 Send the kite, edge and release off your back foot last. At the same time, look and throw your head forwards.

2 Tuck up your legs and throw your head into a forward rotation.

3 Grab the heeled tail of the board and change your head to look beyond and over your rear shoulder to help to continue your rotation.

4 Drop your back hand as this helps to open your body for landing and look where you wish to land.

5 Extend your legs and pull on the front hand hard to redirect the kite forwards.

6 From this point, you can choose to continue in your current direction or under lap the kite to move into a transition.

12

Equipment

12

Equipment

Now you've mastered the basics and more, it's likely you'll be ready to invest in your own equipment. This chapter covers all the kit required – from its manufacture and structure to the pros and cons of the various types within each category.

MANUFACTURING

The cottage industry of local sail-makers that the sports of windsurfing and yachting support does not exist for kites. Instead, they are built in a small number of Asian factories, primarily in China, Sri Lanka and Thailand, with less than 10 per cent being built outside these large production set-ups. The reason for this is that three-dimensional LEI and ram-air kites are reasonably technical to assemble and build, and require precision cutting, sewing and shaping that is far more effectively done on large computer-aided machines than by hand.

This really dictates the market and has resulted in larger brands growing and maintaining ongoing products and design innovation. Ranges and new releases are planned months in advance and made in tens and hundreds. Some of the parts are manufactured in completely different countries and brought together on an assembly line, much like cars, albeit on a far smaller scale in terms of numbers. In addition, a few kite designers have the facility to tweak designs on their local sail tables, meaning they can alter canopy drafts, bridle attachment points and repair damages and larger canopy tears.

Boards, on the other hand, are different and follow both manufacturing paths. Like kites, a large percentage of boards, especially twin-tips, are built in computer-aided factories in Eastern Europe, America and the Far East. With compression mouldings and computer numerical control (CNC) cutting machines, the precision and speed with which a board can be made is remarkable, and results in real value for money for entry-level twin-tips. Some composite sandwich (surfboard-type) boards, however, do keep local 'shapers' alive and kicking with stronger, faster surfboard and foilboard designs being manually produced on a bespoke basis. This also allows technology, R&D, design and evolution to travel much faster on a local scale, rather than waiting for factory prototypes to arrive, be tested, redesigned, resent and retested.

An example of this was plain to see in course racing, where boards went from 45cm (18in) to 70cm (27.5in) in width within two years as the local shapers in hotbed areas such as San Francisco were pushed by leading competitors to gain the latest design edge and podium places. Some larger brands have also taken this opportunity to the next stage by implementing mini

▲ **Board shaping is a technical and artistic skill.**

production facilities at their headquarters to allow them to produce, test and modify new designs very quickly, guaranteeing the best product from the factory when it goes on general release.

There is nothing quite like having your own board shaped for you by a local shaper, who will take care over a design that is personal to you while telling stories of storms and big days they faced before your time. I personally am moved and thrilled by the fact that kiteboarding can help fuel this mini-industry of talented local board producers the world over.

KNOWING WHAT'S RIGHT FOR YOU

Equipment has come a long way in the last decade of kiteboarding and modern kit boasts wide wind ranges so kites can be used in varied wind conditions. Safety systems, which are an integral part of a kite bar or control system, have been much improved by advances in materials and technology, and now carry an ISO Standard (21853), which ensures effective functionality of the release reload systems. Boards range greatly in terms of size, from less than 1m to almost 1m, and from under 5 litres to over 50 litres. Wood, plastic, foam, air, carbon and glassfibre boards are available, in varied designs and shapes. The diversity is both fantastic and confusing.

So where do we start when it comes equipment? It is a bit of a minefield, since of course every manufacturer tells you that their product is the best in every way. In this section I am going to dissect the equipment and explain the different generic types along with some merits and demerits. Having spent the last few years as the test-editor for a leading UK kiteboarding magazine, I have had the pleasure (and occasional hardship) of trying out a fair amount of equipment. I have come to the conclusion that, firstly, everything has improved beyond measure in this time, and secondly, every piece of kit is good for someone somewhere.

I tend to liken equipment to cars, as this is an easy analogy for most people to relate to. As such, there are kites that are Fiestas or Clios, which are cheap, economic and great first-time cars and urban runarounds. Then there are Jaguar and Audi saloons, which cruise the motorways in silent comfort and offer gadgets galore. And then there are rugged off-roaders, blisteringly quick Subarus and countless other types in between.

All you have to do when it comes to selecting your kite, board and indeed harness for that matter, is look at yourself, how and where you are likely to kite, and your goals for the near future. There is of course budget to consider too, but this is often the easiest factor to overcome since second-hand year-old models are now readily available through good retailers. Hiring kit could be a long-term option for someone who wants to carry on kiteboarding when they can, but may not have the money to buy, space to store, or opportunity to use kit frequently enough to warrant the outlay.

Kitefoiling has added a new dimension to the average quiver and has shaken up the large kite market with lighter, single or even no strut LEI type lightwind kites. Not to mention the Olympic racing movement, which represents a reasonable amount of country funded athletes touring the world on the world circuit and progressing the quality and performance of high-speed ram air kites, boards and foils.

TYPES OF KITE

There is one particular type of kite that is far more popular among kiteboarders than any other: the leading edge inflatable (LEI) or tube kite. Invented by the Legaignoux brothers in the early 1990s, it now makes up around 95 per cent of the market for people kiteboarding on water. Almost all the manufacturers, of which there are now lots, produce a whole range of LEI kites, from strong- to light-wind sizes and with models for different disciplines of competition and genres of the sport. I go into more detail on LEIs on page 152.

On instructor-training courses I often set new students a game of 'kiteboard boggle', for which separate groups must think of as many kiteboarding-specific companies as they can. The team with the longest, unique list wins. Some student groups came up with over 100 companies making specific kiteboarding, and now winging, equipment. I always think this massive growth and diversity of brands is very positive for a sport as it pushes on innovation and development and creates jobs.

There are also two other generic kite types, but in terms of numbers sold these pale into insignificance.

FRAME KITES

I always compare this type of kite to Batman's wing. They have solid spars or battens usually made from fibreglass, wood or carbon, which fit together to make a frame. The canopy, which is almost always a single skin, is stretched over this frame.

Small toy kites are commonly frame kites, the classic being the diamond kite, which most children around the world will recognise and will probably have tried to fly at some point. The category also includes all manner of delta and three-dimensional designs, which are often flown in synchrony at kite-flying festivals in displays and shows.

Frame kites are no longer used for kiteboarding, although Peter Lynn, a manufacturer from New Zealand did produce the infamous 'C-Quad' in the late 1990s, which had a fantastic ability to sink and create the biggest 'bird's nest' with the lines in record time...

FOIL KITES

These kites represent 100 per cent of the kitefoiling racing scene. They won the performance battle in around 2015 and have streaked ahead in lightwind performance over LEI ever since. Only a handful of manufacturers are registering kites for the Olympic class of kitefoil racing. This is unique among all the sailing classes where every other class is one design. Namibian deserts and American salt plains witnessed bizarre antics between the 1960s and 1990s, when land speed attempts were made using three-wheeled buggies, unicycles and various wheeled craft, which were dragged around at breakneck/leg and arm speeds.

A foil kite, or ram-air as it could technically be described, has no solid material inside it to provide shape or structure. Instead they have two skins, top and bottom, which are sewn together to create a three-dimensional shape that has inner cells to reduce distortion. The leading edge of these kites is generally open to some degree, although modern versions have flaps to reduce

▲ Foil kite.

▲ C-kite.

▲ Cabrinha bow kite.

▲ Hybrid kite.

water ingress if accidentally crashed. These open cells allow the air to 'ram' in and fill the canopy. Once in the air they are supported by a reasonably complex set of bridle lines, which are configured in triangular series and connected to the underside of the canopy in lots of measured places. Once a foil is flying the bridles and kite look completely uniform, creating a very efficient and graceful shape, although on the ground they look like a badly landed folded parachute.

Foil kites are far more efficient at generating power than LEI kites. They also weigh less and are generally more stable. They can be unpacked, launched, landed and stowed again independently without the need for any assistance or connecting of lines. A 5m (16ft) foil kite would be comparable in power terms to an 8.5m (28ft) LEI kite. Racers will frequently use 21m² foil kites for lightwind racing. This is a modest paragliding size of wing albeit very different in shape and purpose. There is a growing recreational foiling market for intermediates and those wanting lightwind performance. There is still a slight cost barrier to foil kites as they tend to be 10–30 per cent more expensive than equivalent purposed LEIs.

On land, most kite schools will introduce basic kite-flying skills using a small foil kite on a bar or handles. They are also the popular choice for snow, landboard and buggy disciplines, as the relaunch is not a problem on solid ground. Foil kites are also commonplace for playing with in the park, and as a category they include all forms of paraglider and parachute, which are variations on the same design.

LEI/TUBE KITES

We found out where LEI kites came from in the first chapter of this book, but what exactly are they? LEI or tube kites gain their shape, which can differ dramatically, from a series of pressurised tubes or struts that are attached to the rear of a curved leading edge tube. The majority of LEIs have three struts, some larger more performance orientated models have five and a new breed of single strut and no strut models are gaining popularity for kitefoiling in lighter airs.

These tubes are inflated to high psi levels using a foot pump before each session in order to provide stability and reduce distortion to a minimum through the kite. The average psi levels are around 6–10.

Modern LEIs are inflated through a singular valve on the leading edge, which pushes the air through one-way valves into the struts. The struts can then be locked off so a puncture will only affect the section it is in. Once inflated, they provide good structure for the single canopy skin that is stretched over the skeleton. This is invaluable when the kite crashes as it prevents it from sinking and also allows the kite to hold its shape and consequently

HOW BIG IS AN LEI?

LEIs are measured in terms of area, usually square metres, in the same way a carpet-fitter would measure a room. This was not always the case; early designers at Wipika measured their kites in 'projected' area, which was the surface area of the underside of the kite that was exposed to the wind when flying. This is a far more precise and technical measurement, and for a number of years companies battled over whether to use surface or projected area measurements when it came to sizing and advertising their products. Naish was the early supporter and purveyor of surface area measurements, as this is what they used for their windsurf sail measurements. Wipika, however, stuck by the projected measurement. By 2006 or 2007 the battle was over and surface area measurements became the standard, primarily because the main manufacturers and brands were also making windsurfing sails and wanted consistency within their brands.

take off again. A good modern learning LEI will take off reliably in a matter of seconds in the right wind.

LEI kites have progressed from One, the original C kite, through defined revolutions of the 'bow' kite to a range these days of delta hybrid kites which are all coming together in a more mellow profile and mixture of bridles configurations.

There are still a few distinct types, and there are definitely different strokes for different folks and disciplines, but all kites need to do a few common things: generate power, steer efficiently, relaunch if they crash and deliver smooth motion and power control.

C-KITES

The original inflatable kites were designed in a C-shaped arc and subsequently the name has stuck. Today, this design characteristic is primarily used by kiters wishing to excel in the freestyle discipline. The kites boast great dynamic power, lift and 'boost' by holding lots of wind in the very curved profile shape, which also gives good stability when the rider is unhooked from the chickenloop.

They are not the easiest type of kite to fly, control or relaunch because of their defined curvature of leading edge, and higher average aspect ratio. I would compare traditional progressive C-kites with a Subaru Impreza, Renault Clio Williams or a Ford Escort RS Cosworth (for

▼ **Wakestyle.**

those of us who can remember those!). The latest breed of aggressive C-kites now boasts mini bridles on the front power lines, which aid depower, steering and relaunch.

BOW KITES

2006 was the year in which the first early bow kites emerged and Cabrinha as a brand marketed this kite revolution with their 'one kite from 10–30 knots of breeze'. A bow kite has a far less curved profile to the leading edge than that of a C-kite; they are more like an archer's bow in profile. To stabilise this far flatter profile a series of bridles were initially commonplace to support the leading edge. Hence you may hear the term supported leading edge (SLE) kite used, especially when referring to models made between 2007 and 2011.

Bow kites have a very effective depower capability, which means they can cope with large wind ranges. This increased trimming control allows the pilot to alter the angle of attack to a near-negative angle, thus spilling all the lifting power from the canopy.

The flatter profile also allows them to fly very efficiently and more towards the front of the wind window, which is why they are popular with racing and speed disciplines. They are not as stable as C-kites when unhooked and can stall or over-sheet. In car terms, bow kites are Audi A8 Saloons, Mercedes E-Class and BMW 5 and 7 Series models – fast, smooth, technical and refined pedigree products for the discerning customer.

▼ **Ready to launch.**

HYBRID KITES

Is this the most recent genre to be defined within the LEI camp? The point is debatable. Hybrid kites have been around since 2008/9 and combine the good points of C-kites and bow kites to produce a very effective all-rounder. They often boast a leading-edge profile similar to that of modern C-kites but the leading edge then sweeps round in a curve rather than the 90-degree wing tip corner found on a C-kite. Hybrid kites also have a semi-supported leading edge where bridles will support the wing tips and sides of the leading edge but will not meet in the middle.

Many kites fall broadly within this category in modern design terms and there is nothing to say where the line is between types, other than a manufacturer's pitch. A good hybrid kite will boast good wind range, trimming and control, while also being able to pop, boost and unhook well. It is therefore a popular choice for the modern kiteboarder who wants to do a bit of everything in a mix of winds but doesn't want to buy three kites in the same size for three different types of conditions.

ASPECT RATIO

Along with projected area sizing, the early days between 1998 and 2005 saw kites also being marketed and sold on the basis of their aspect ratio. The most famous of these was the legendary Naish AR5 (Aspect Ratio 5).

Aspect ratio is simply the sum of the length of the leading edge divided by the length along the centre strut or point of the kite from leading to trailing edge. A figure less than 4.5 was generally regarded as being medium to low, with 3 being low. Kites with a lower aspect ratio were deeper from front to back and narrower from tip to tip. This made them more stable and easier to fly and relaunch. Kites with an aspect ratio of 5 or more were high.

There was a time, as kites evolved towards the extreme at such a speed, when pub talk would consist of a form of Top Trumps using competing aspect ratios. An aspect ratio of more than 6 guaranteed free beer all night. Kite design has not slowed down, but has become more

evolutionary rather than revolutionary in recent years. What is of significant change is the materials going into kites.

Most kites are made from polyester, in fact the large majority use a Teijin fabric produced by one company for most of the canopy material. Mylar, Dacron and even neoprene reinforcements are also commonplace on the outer edge and tubular areas. In recent years new materials are being experimented with like Aluula to both increase strength and reduce stretch and weight. The arms race towards the ultimate fabric is only going to be accelerated by kiteboarding's Olympic inclusion as the first-past-the-post, or over the line in this case, will surely be on the lightest, strongest, stiffest kite available.

TYPES OF BOARD

Just like kites, boards come in all shapes and sizes. However, unlike kites, in the last few years boards have exploded in variety of shape, construction and diversity. The fact you can have a go at making your own board in the garage obviously helps and celebrates cottage industry custom shapers developing boards for specific purposes. This has, in no small part, helped kitefoil board development progress rapidly from large ungainly surfboard type designs to the modern tiny tray type styles that frequent lightwind beaches worldwide.

The most popular type of board used by kiteboarders is still the twin-tip, although not by much, as surfboard production is currently nearing equal numbers, (this might simply be due to twin-tips being so strong and robust that riders are keeping them longer and buying a new surfboard instead). The twin-tip was invented in 1999 by Franz Olry, and was responsible in part for bringing a huge wave of new people into kiteboarding, as it suddenly became easy to turn around and edge effectively. This was also helped by the 4-line control bar system, which was launched around the same time.

Board design and experimentation over the last decade has been colourful, eccentric and diverse, and this has led to the evolution of defined disciplines within the sport and the emergence of very different board types, constructions and designs. The fact that you can have a go at building a board in the garage at home with a bit of know-how and some basic tools and materials aids this. Kites, on the other hand, have been almost exclusively factory-produced since day one, due to the complex nature of their design and construction.

This section explains the generic types of boards available and their design characteristics and typical constructions, while the next chapter examines the disciplines of the sport in more depth and looks at how they are used, and by whom, at all levels.

TWIN-TIPS

The twin-tip board is the most popular type of kiteboard. It is symmetrical at both ends and has a designated windward (heelside) rail, and toeside or leeward rail opposite. Generally these two rails will be symmetrical in outline. Twin-tips range greatly in size, shape and construction. A kiteboarder should consider his or her own size, level and aspirations when selecting the right one. The average size to begin with is around 140cm (55in) in length and roughly 40cm (16in) in width at the widest point.

Twin-tips are good for freestyle and general fun-riding in flat, bumpy and wavy conditions, from light to strong winds. Their biggest selling point is their ease of turning, as the rider does not have to switch their feet when changing direction. They are also the most suitable type of board to use for learning to jump, rotate and move into freestyle. The average length of boards used to become progressively smaller towards 125cm (49in) for proficient riders, but the last two or three years has seen advanced board lengths creep towards 140 (55in) and far more freestyle riders fitting wakeboard-style boots to their boards.

The freestyle elite and those on the world tour now almost exclusively use wakeboard bindings in order to be competitive and perform the in-vogue move. These bindings are now produced by kiteboard manufacturers, which is a recent evolution as standard wakeboard bindings were the only available type just a few years ago. These bindings are often fitted to a standard all-round/progressive twin-tip and there are also dedicated bindings-only boards. The cost of the bindings is greater than that of standard footstraps, but then so is the level of support and power they provide the rider.

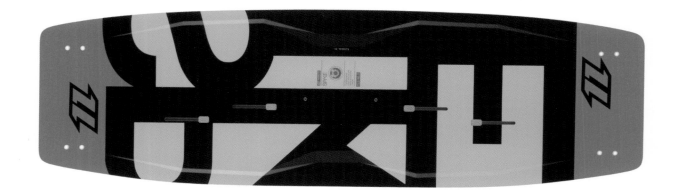

▲ **A regular twin-tip board.**

SPEED BOARDS Far less popular but no less important are speed boards. These are often not a true twin-tip as they are asymmetrical (on a sided-riding bias) but they fit better into the twin-tip category than any other. These boards are no-compromise designs built for one purpose: speed. Everything about them is aimed at going fast. Most speed courses, like the Namibian trench I mentioned earlier, are built to ride on one tack only, with the course set on a broad reach. The Lüderitz trench is set to ride starboard tack, which is worth knowing so you avoid turning up with a board set up for a port tack course.

Speed boards are almost impossible to ride, turn or even float at slower speeds or in bumpy water, which makes getting back up to the top of the run a long and painful process in the heavy winds needed for setting records.

MUTANTS These are far less popular today than they were in their heyday of the early 2000s, when they were the must-have board on the freestyle world tour. A mutant is a twin-tip board with two footstraps that don't require you to switch your feet, and fins at both ends, except there is a bias towards one end. Their non-symmetrical design means they perform better in one direction – for jumping, riding a wave, going fast etc – but would also work to travel back in the other direction without the need for performing a gybe or tack requiring you to switch your feet, which can lead to falls and wipeouts. In the right conditions, which could be windy cross-onshore or mushy wavy conditions, mutants can excel, making it easy to get out through the bumps, turn quickly and reliably between waves, boost and still land in either direction. Despite this, they have lost favour in recent years, with many companies not including one in their current line-ups. But watch this space, as I suspect their day will return.

DOOR One final type of twin-tip that deserves a mention as a partial sub-category of twin-tips is the light-wind 'Door.' These boards are standard, symmetrically shaped twin-tips, still with two straps and four fins, but they have been stretched in design and, as their name suggests, resemble the shape of a door. The merit of these rectangular boards is purely that they can be used to get a novice kiteboarder riding prolonged distances easily, since with far more edge and surface area they can get up and go very early and novices are forgiven minor mistakes in kite-piloting, planing through lulls and at very low speeds. Modern technology has introduced carbon and lightweight materials to these designs, which are

sometimes used by intermediates as well as beginners as light-wind alternatives to more technical directionals and as a cheaper option than buying a very large kite.

DIRECTIONALS

In the same way that 'twin-tips' encapsulate speed, mutants, wakeboards and Doors, 'directionals' is a broad term that includes wave- and surf-orientated boards both with straps and without, raceboards, freerace boards and foilboards. A smaller percentage of the current market is made up of directional boards, but only just, and quite possibly this balance could tip in the near future.

WAVE BOARDS These represent the majority of boards in the directional camp, with manufacturers producing dreamy ranges from small, squat, fishtail fun-boards, to sleek, long, no-compromise big-wave guns for the fearless watermen taking on the outer Hawaiian and European reefs during winter storms. These ranges tempt and entice you with beautiful wood finishes and elegant graphics that look so good in a garaged quiver. Or is that just me?

In shape, style and fin configuration they resemble scaled-down (average size 1.8m (5ft 11in)) surfboards that have been beefed up in terms of construction. This is not surprising as their purpose is to ride waves. In fact there is no reason for not grabbing an old (or indeed new) standard surfboard and taking it for a spin. They can be ridden with one, two or no straps. The general trend currently on the kiteboarding world tour is strapless riding, which has gained the sport major credibility within the surfing community and introduced a whole new repertoire of must-do strapless airs and tricks, for which extreme skill is required in order to maintain contact with the board.

The waves now being ridden with kites and strapless surfboards are comparable to the most challenging surf breaks on the global scene, with wave venues such as Teahupo'o (Tahiti), Jaws (Maui), Mavericks (Northern California) and occasionally Pipeline (Hawaii) being ridden, and tube riding being the new goal of the elite.

The merit of a specific kite-waveboard over a standard surfboard comes down to construction. A normal 170g (6oz) fibreglass surfboard with FCS fin mountings will not stand up to the increased load applied by the rider edging constantly against the kite; the board will become dented with foot compressions and finboxes will often fail. Specific kite-waveboards are built more substantially

▲ **Fun wave (strapless) freestyle board.**

to combat these extra stresses, especially since large strapless airs and tricks are now being practised. The shape of a dedicated kite-waveboard will also tend to be thinner top to bottom, with narrower rails and a flatter rear section, all of which allow the board to be ridden faster and more aggressively, as is the kite when it is introduced.

SKIMBOARDS

The definition of a skimboard used to be a wooden disk of hardwood with very few design features, which was thrown into a shore-break or along very shallow water mostly by young, enthusiastic riders who would run after it, jump on and skim along for a few metres of self-generated momentum, before sinking or crashing into the next wave. This 'sport' is possibly the purveyor of the 'banana-skin wipeout', which is when a skimboarder has too much weight leaning back and, on jumping on to the board, falls backwards dramatically, legs up, head down, projecting the board forwards and wiping out.

Kiteboarding has dabbled with skimboards for a decade or so and numerous manufacturers have a model in their range. They are not performance-orientated boards and are built for fun and playing around. They are thin from top to bottom and often simple in construction, with very shallow

🔺 **A skimboard**

fins or sometimes none at all. Their directional disc-type shape gives them good surface area, which allows them to be easy to use in light winds. I often have one lying on the beach during clinics so that it is easy for pupils to come in, grab it and go and play for a few minutes to relax, enjoy and break up the pounding involved when learning twin-tip tricks and physical directional training.

🔺 **A wave board.**

HYDROFOILS

The most recently recognised discipline of kiteboarding currently mushrooming among the racing circuit, foilboarding is the in-vogue craze to have a go at. The fin is the most important part of the foilboard: it is 90 per cent fin and 10 per cent board. It first appeared on the scene in the early 2000s, when Laird Hamilton carried out numerous experiments and made some great videos of himself blasting around on ocean swells in alpine snowboard boots and bindings on a hydrofoil board. Various pockets of kiteboarders around the world subsequently played around and had a go. I remember there was very limited success with the technical mounting points for the boots, and the boards' extreme weight made transporting them a real challenge. It was also hard to find a suitable venue. Modern foilboards are now mostly ridden without straps, and the board is simply an old tiny surfboard or skimboard that is just large enough to stand on in order to propel the fin along for a moment until it rises from the water and supplies lift and motion all on its own. The America's Cup has brought the potential of modern hydrofoil sailing craft into the public eye with huge budgets, speeds, and incredible Formula One-type sailing racing. In parallel to this, kite hydrofoil racing now has a World Cup circuit, recognised class and an avid following of expert competitors. While it will never become anything more than a niche class, the growing interest and progressively more user-friendly equipment means that it is encouraging intermediates with access to suitable locations to have a go. The serene experience of floating quietly above the water that the sport offers, combined with the board's incredible light-wind performance, means it is becoming more and more enticing.

▼ ▶ **Hydrofoil is a technical and high performance new discipline of kiteboarding. Riding the foil is unique and serene, floating above the water's surface.**

▲ Night kiting.

BARS

All kiteboarding kites are flown using using a bar or 'control system' that usually has four lines connecting it to the kite, harnessing the power and providing steerage. Control bars have many generic parts and all possess key essential features such as a safety leash, chickenloop release system, and trim or sheeting system. However, there is a huge variety of designs among these systems, some of which are better than others. I am often surprised when I am testing equipment just how good, or indeed bad, some of the modern control bar systems are. I repeatedly say to students, fellow kiters and clients on clinic trips that a new control bar, unwrapped by yourself, isn't 'safe' until you have examined it and understood and learned how it works.

LINES

Without doubt the most expensive and most dangerous part of a control bar is the lines. The average length of lines supplied with most modern kites is 20–25m (66–82ft). The lines are usually made from spectra, a technical rope that is very strong and does not stretch a noticeable amount. Technically it does stretch a very small amount, usually laminar among lines on a given bar, but the effect is minimal. By way of comparison, just imagine tensioning 25m (82ft) of mainsheet halyard from a sailing yacht; the line would almost act like a spring. The average breaking strain is 200–400kg (440–880lb) in weight, which is a phenomenal amount, and also raises same safety concerns.

The first thing a kiteboarding instructor learns about equipment on their training course is how strong and potentially dangerous the lines can be. A wise rule to apply throughout your kiteboarding career is not to wrap or let kite lines get wrapped around any part of your body. It is too strong to break with your hands and is very thin, so can cut through harnesses, wetsuits and skin very efficiently.

Unlike early line sets, which snapped frequently, modern lines rarely break unless they are repeatedly knotted, or subjected to fraying due to friction. The quality and durability of these lines is a testament to modern materials and technology.

THE CONTROL BAR

Every time you go kiteboarding you will spend the entire time connected to the control bar; even unhooking freestylers will attach a leash to prevent it from blowing away if they drop it. Bars are made from aluminum and carbon and are covered in varying colours and patterns of soft rubber grip. Spaces for line-winding at both ends have now been made into a design feature with bungees to secure it all. A hole in the centre allows the trim system to work seamlessly.

CHICKENLOOP The chickenloop is an essential and integral part of a control bar. The early days of 2-line kites led to the chickenloop gaining its name, since riders who used its depowerable 4-line system were referred to as 'chickens'. The chickenloop attaches the pilot to the kite via the harness, which I will explain in more detail shortly. Regardless of type, size and material they are all designed to release from the harness, letting the kite flag on to one or two of the remaining lines, which depowers the kite. Most chickenloops also have a 'donkey dick' (or 'donkey tail' if you want to be more polite). This slots down between the chickenloop and harness hook to prevent the chickenloop falling off if the lines go slack momentarily. The reloading of chickenloop release systems is now improving rapidly, which makes it feasible to reassemble and relaunch in water.

In recent years the chickenloop has evolved to incorporate different methods of attachment. It is now not uncommon for waveriders who have no intention of unhooking to connect their chickenloop to a rope on their harness. No hook exists in these systems, and they have an ergonomic advantage of allowing the centre of effort to move across your abdomen as your hips move. They also prevent accidental unhooking of the chickenloop, which is very useful.

▲▼ The bar system in use.

PULL SYSTEMS These must be pulled towards the pilot to activate the release. Often they have a flapped Velcro design. These were among the earliest types of chickenloop and are becoming antiquated today in comparison to more mechanical push-away systems. The main disadvantage with a pull system is that it requires tension to be activated, which is not always possible if a kite has crashed strangely and needs to be released.

PUSH-AWAY SYSTEMS These comprise the majority of the modern market and, although they come in all different shapes, colours and sizes, they must all be grabbed with one or both hands and pushed away from the pilot to release. They are often mechanical and spring-loaded, which makes releasing very easy. The ISO 21853 Standard that was implemented in 2019 dictates that no more than 5kg (11lb) of applied pressure must be required to activate the release system with either one or both hands. Pushing away means there is no need for line tension and the system can be released in any situation. A number of other criteria around the activation ease, reloading and functionality is identified in this Standard and testing is undertaken on all bars before certification is issued.

TRIMLINE

Most, but not all, trimming or sheeting systems reside above the bar and are an arm's reach away at the top of the bar-throw trimming section. The purpose of the trim strap is similar to that of the mainsheet on a yacht. It can be adjusted, then fixed in position, to provide the most advantageous angle of attack for the kite on a given day. The more wind or power you have the more trim you will apply to your kite to depower it. If you are fully trimmed in/depowered, and your kite is still too powerful you need to change down a kite size.

Various clam cleats, webbing straps and locking cleats are used. Good systems are ergonomically designed and easy to adjust on the move. A racer may adjust their trim straps numerous times throughout a race, depending on their heading.

SAFETY LEASH

Another piece of mandatory equipment is the safety leash. This is a spring-loaded strong cord, which now usually attaches to the side or rear of your harness. It is then connected to the safety line on the kite. When a chickenloop is released, the kite is flagged preferably on to one but sometimes two lines, which cannot power up the kite. All leashes will have a clip at one end to allow quick and easy attachment to the kite's safety line, and a push-away release at the other to allow the pilot to detach completely from the kite if absolutely necessary. It is very expensive and potentially dangerous for people downwind to release the kite altogether. Modern freestyle leashes can resemble a snake wrapping around the rider, and are often brightly coloured.

Many foilers, racers and waveriders may use a shorter leash, attached to the front of their harness, as they have no need for the extra length that a freestyler requires to handle pass the bar when unhooked.

RIDING SUICIDE

This is a term used to describe attaching your safety leash to your chickenloop or trimline. It derives from the fact that years ago this was not such a great idea. The term has stuck, but the modern leashing attachments mean it is perfectly safe, and is a far quicker leashing system for advanced freestyle moves with suitably modern depowerable kites.

4- AND 5-LINE BARS

There tend to be two types of people in kiteboarding: 4-liners and 5-liners. I personally like and frequently use both systems. For teaching I am an advocate of the 5th-line system as it guarantees 100 per cent depower and aids relaunching in extremely light wind.

4-LINE BARS The main merit of a 4-line control bar system is that there is less line, and indeed air friction. It is less likely to tangle and, if it does, it can easily be ridden home with a minor tangle. For these simple reasons they make up the greater market share. Some systems do not flag on to a single line, meaning complete depower is occasionally compromised, and should not be used by beginners. In reality however, they are widely used by beginners although manufacturers are changing and improving every year.

5-LINE BARS These bars were a revolutionary invention around 2004–5. They gave complete depower in an age when kites were not easily depowered and released safely. They also dramatically improved relaunching capabilities, which at the time was a big issue for the high-aspect-ratio C-kite designs of the era. Today, 5-line bars are still a very popular choice and provide excellent safety, relaunch potential and added stability without

the need for more extensive bridles. The downside is that they can be trickier to limp home on with twisted lines, which in certain environments with more lines is a potential occurrence.

THE RIGHT KIT FOR YOU

All of these sections build up quite an extensive picture of modern hardware. As I mentioned at the beginning, there is no 'best kite in the world', just the best one for you. So, decide what features you want, how much you want to spend and where you want it to take you, then have a look. Ask instructors (their advice is invaluable) and consult friends, shops and the Internet. Then make a sensible decision about your new toys. Just remember, you might want a Range Rover more than anything, but it could be completely the wrong car for you when what you need is a Ford Fiesta.

▼ **The 5-line bar system.**

▲ **Approaching the start line, foil race training.**

FOILING

Kiteboarding has come a long way since publication of the first edition of this book, way back when I was experimenting with foiling by bolting random foils onto unsuitable boards to see how they worked (or didn't!). Now, in the upcoming Paris 2024 Olympics, five of the eight medals for sailing are in foiling disciplines: IQfoil windsurf men and women, the Nacra mixed multihull and kiteboarding men and women.

Foiling has truly captured the sailing world, with countless brands, disciplines and all manner of crazy antics being attempted, from big wave tube riding on foils to unhooked freestyle kitefoiling and wingfoiling.

There is now a genre of foiling in almost all forms of watersport, from surf foiling in waves, downwinder foiling, SUP foiling, windsurf foiling, foiling dinghies like moths and wasps, kitefoiling and the latest watersports craze to go viral – wingfoiling, where the pilot holds a (currently) inflatable wing like a sail for power and stands on a foiling board to ride.

All of this, as I alluded to in the first edition of this book, was courtesy of high-performance big boat racing like the America's Cup and SailGP, where deep pocketed trillionaires fuel sailing teams to duel at speeds of up to 50+ knots on large Formula One type foiling sailing boats.

So why all this crazy infatuation for riding on 'a bag of knives' as my dad likes to call them? Well, who wouldn't like to ride silently and serenely above the surface of the water, riding with a perfect constant and stable medium (solid water), allowing you to cruise upwind (and downwind) at previously impossible angles, allowing far faster racing, exploring further and more enjoyment in lower wind speeds? Foiling has really taken hold in European waters where it is commonplace to have 10–20 knots of wind and large, flat deep areas of open water, which are fairly mundane for proficient practitioners on standard planing craft after a while. But jump on a foil and there are a host of new skills and tricks to master, along with making it far easier to hold your ground and go upwind, which is the classic challenge for all kiteboarders, especially in light winds, eliminating the 'walk of shame' back up the beach.

In fact, the new challenge can sometimes be getting back downwind, as foils are so efficient to windward. Giving rise to the 'stride of pride' back down the beach, as a fellow coach and good pal calls it. So how do they work? The basics are fairly straightforward, and not actually that new. The sharper end becomes very techy very quickly, so let's stay simple for now.

ANATOMY OF A WING

The foil bolts onto the underside of the board, there is a track and plate system that most manufacturers are using, allowing a bit of interchangeability among products. Although racing currently uses a different finbox system.

The mast then points down vertically from the board, these vary in length between around 0.5–1m (1.6–3.3ft). The fuselage bolts onto the bottom of the mast, these also vary in length between 0.45–0.8m (1.5–2.6ft) In length, both can be either aluminium or carbon. The front wing attaches to the front of the fuse and the stabiliser at the rear, similar to an aeroplane. These wing also vary dramatically in size, shape, profile and materials.

Once the board starts moving the front wing creates lift, if countered by a downforce pressure from the pilot the board will rise up onto the foil with the wings below the surface and the board above the water. The faster you go, the more lift you create and stability (provided you keep the wings under the surface of the water).

As you can imagine this all takes a bit of skill and balance, although not that much. In the last five years especially, equipment has become far easier and more controllable to learn with, progress with which has made it very accessible for your normal guys and girls to master. As with all sailing boardsports, if you can master the corners, you will get hooked, and the birth of larger, lower aspect ratio wings, short masts and stable voluminous boards has helped hugely. Along with teaching and coaching systems developing and improving

▼ **Beating upwind off the line, kitefoil racing.**

over time, along with more people able to deliver safe tuition.

I truly am genuinely excited to see where the foiling elements of our sport is going to take us. With a shop window like the Olympics to show off these new supercharged sailing disciplines we could see a real surge in activity and popularity, not just for kiting but windsurfing, wingsurfing and the other smaller foiling craft, and all without the need for a supporting trillionaire.

WINGING

Winging, wingfoiling, wingsurfing whatever you call it, you cannot deny, it is happening. It's new but not actually that new, as foils have been around for decades in certain forms, and I for one had a 'WindWing' in 2002, which was a solid version of the new inflatable ones of today. It is more a meeting of technologies and disciplines that has created this new-fangled craze.

Being an avid water person, I of course got on to this craze early and, just like kiting in the early days, I ignored all the good advice (and indeed equipment) and jumped on a far too advanced rig in strong winds and rough seas and proceeded to learn... the hard way. After a year or so of flirting with it, and a Covid winter at home putting in the hours, I had it cracked, only to see all the lovely new easy-to-learn equipment arrive a year later, about the same time as I wrote the training system for it, which makes it a pleasure to learn these days.

Winging has two emerging forms. Wingsurfing is the non-foiling displacement board version, which is both easy to learn and fab for all, young and old. It is gaining huge traction in outdoor centres nationwide as a great kids and adult activity session for all abilities. This is of course great as it fuels the second version: Wingfoiling. This uses exactly the same wing-/sail-for-power generation by capturing the wind. But the board is smaller and has a foil on the bottom. Boards can vary greatly in size shape and volume just like the foils, but

having had a few seasons of teaching and coaching in this new arena, I think it has potential as it is quicker than kitefoiling to learn and far more transportable than windsurf foiling. It also doesn't require such high 'quality' wind, hence it can be practiced inland on lakes and areas with gustier winds where kites struggle to go.

Already in a couple of seasons new pro wingers and manufacturers have pushed the sport to incredible levels. Young freestylers are performing triple pirouette rotations including wing passes and landing back on the foil. The front and back loop have been perfected in competitions, and waveriding has gone into the big wave and tube riding arena with a vengeance.

So how you get into this new craze, well just like all these watersports, with some professional lessons at a reputable school. It just so happens that I wrote the world's first wingfoil and wingsurfing scheme with a good pal and expert coach Sam Ross. This British Kitesports Association (BKSA) and British Stand Up Paddleboarding Association (BSUPA) scheme set a bit of a benchmark and is now used in schools across the UK. We also assisted the Royal Yachting Association (RYA) in the development of their scheme and now the three bodies cross recognise each other's schemes to a degree which allows instructors to transition between recognised centres and convert their licenses easily.

Around the world systems are being developed for both wingsurf and wing foil. It is easy safe and super fun to learn and arguably the quickest way to getting foiling on a wind powered craft.

The learning process starts on land with a wing, mastering rig control, power and neutral positions, moving and turning the wing. It then progresses onto the water on a displacement board with a centreboard, similar to a beginner windsurfing board. Learning to along on your knees and then standing, turning and onto upwind, downwind sailing tacks and gybes.

Once you have got to grips with wingsurfing, which could be the goal and is a great fun activity in itself. You can then progress onto a voluminous wingfoil board. The rough size could be gauged on twice your body weight in kgs in litres of volume. This will enable you to stand fairly comfortably riding the board off the foil. Then comes the 'rise and glide' where as your speed increases the foil begins to work and create lift to rise you up above the water.

Of course there's a few wipe-outs along the way but this stage can realistically be attained in two to three sessions. From then on in its all down to how much practice one puts in, the more time on the water in varied locations the more you will progress.

It will be interesting to see where this new craze ends up in another decade as the possibilities are quite extensive, given that with a lower quality of wind required a lot more locations around the world both coastal and inland.

▼ **Wingfoiling.**

SOFTWARE

As if deciding which kite, board and bar to buy wasn't enough to confuse you, there's a whole other collection of equipment that's essential for comfort and support, which I term as 'software'.

WETSUITS

Coming from northern Europe, I have grown accustomed to wearing a wetsuit and boots, gloves, hats and anything else for that matter in a bid to stay warm in winter while out kiteboarding. As a result of thousands of other people like me who want to get on the water no matter how chilly it is, the wetsuit market in Europe is measured in tens of millions of Euros. In other parts of the globe, such as the Caribbean and the Indonesian archipelago, the need simply isn't there; they have a buoyant sunscreen market instead!

Wetsuits provide warmth by insulating the person wearing it with a layer of water or, in modern suits, air. This liquid or air heats to body temperature. Modern materials and construction have made wetsuits vastly warmer and more comfortable now than when I learned to kiteboard, persisting despite the cold through my first few northern-European winters.

There are numerous companies producing and selling wetsuits, from supermarkets to exclusive fashion and clothing brands. To decide on the best wetsuit, you need to look at where and how you are going to use it. An occasional kiteboarder enjoying the temperate climate of a Californian winter will need perhaps a short leg, long arm spring suit. An active full-time instructor in northern France or the UK in wintertime, on the other hand, will need a 6mm (0.23in) hooded, fluid-seam-welded full winter suit. The best way to find the right wetsuit is to look at four basic qualities:

◄ **It's important to choose the right wetsuit for you. Consider where and how you're going to use it.**

MATERIAL Neoprene comes in a range of different formats. Single-lined neoprene is smooth on one side – the outer skin – making it less susceptible to wind-chill but meaning it can snag more easily. Double-lined neoprene is lined on both sides, making the suit more durable but prone to wind-chill. 'Super stretch' refers to neoprene in which elastic qualities are increased, making it more flexible. A mixture of durable legs, warm abdomen and stretchy arms is a good combination to look out for when choosing an all-round suit.

THICKNESS How thick a wetsuit is directly relates to its warmth: the thicker the suit, the warmer it will be. Be aware, however, that thickness also reduces flexibility and comfort. Thickness ranges from 1–8mm (0.04–0.3in) at the extremes, with 3–5mm (0.12–0.2in) being the best for most all-round suits.

SEAMS Seam and stitching technology have turned modern wetsuits into something more akin to dry suits by sealing and making suits watertight throughout. The only water ingress is through the arms, legs and neck, which are well sealed to the skin. This often results in a person still being dry around the abdomen at the end of a session, which is far more pleasant to experience and stops you expending as much energy on keeping warm.

Basic overlock and flatlock stitching will allow water to leak through a suit's seams. Blind stitching, until stressed or stretched, means the suit is almost completely sealed. Welded and taped seams are watertight even under extreme stretching.

FIT The fit of a wetsuit is, above everything else, the most important consideration; a suit's sealed seams will not help keep out the cold if it fits like a baggy jumper. Wetsuits can seem tight and uncomfortable at first but soon become tolerable, especially once you appreciate the warmth benefits they bring. The phrase 'they will grow into it' is not one to be applied to a winter wetsuit: get one that fits properly.

As you enhance the materials, stitching, thickness and design of a suit it will increase in cost, comfort and performance. Some wetsuits are now very expensive and are overkill for the everyday recreational user. A budget of £150–200 will buy you a warm comfortable suit to get started. Cold winters can sometimes require a range of neoprene accessories to protect the body's extremities. Wetsuit stockists will often sell booties, gloves and hats, which are invaluable in the depths of winter, for prolonging sessions and increasing personal comfort.

Speaking as an instructor, a popular new invention in the last five years is the neoprene overcoat or rigging jacket. Originally designed for windsurfing competitors to put on between racing heats to help combat the wind chill, the first versions looked like menacing trench coats from *The Matrix* in black neoprene with hoods on. These jackets are now made in all manner of colours and designs and have become the must-have accessory of all cold-climate watersports instructors. They are made from double-lined neoprene with basic stitching, and fit loosely over a sandy wet person wearing their harness. They can also be totally submerged and will drain, but serve to trap a layer of air inside and prevent exothermic heat loss from the skintight wetsuit.

RASH VESTS

If you're lucky enough to live in, or frequently visit, subtropical destinations for kiteboarding, then an essential piece of kit is a rash vest. This does not keep you warm, but rather keeps the sun off your skin and reduces chafing around your arms, chest and neck from the harness and general movement. People from colder climes often underestimate the sun, but it is actually a greater hazard than the cold, as its effects sneak up on you and can overwhelm a person with exhaustion and sickness hours after the exposure. This is unlike hyperthermia, which is immediately obvious and requires action at the time. As a result, long-sleeved rash vests, hats and plenty of decent waterproof sunscreen are essential for your tropical kiteboarding experiences.

HARNESSES

There are two types of harness:

SEAT HARNESSES These are the original type of kiteboarding harness. The nappy-style design supports and keeps the hooking point down around your waist when the kite is constantly trying to pull it up, especially when learning. Nowadays they are still common for some beginners and are the consistent choice for all racing, speed and distance competitors because of the lower centre of gravity they provide for these disciplines. They are similar to windsurfing harnesses but have thicker stitching, more reinforcement and a handle/leash attachment point on the side or rear.

WAIST HARNESSES This type of harness is the more popular choice these days as it is more comfortable to wear and easier to move in than seat harnesses. They also look a bit cooler. Again, similar to windsurfing waist harnesses, these sit between the hips and ribs, with a hook around belly-button height. They have pushed the evolution of harnesses as they have become more reinforced and supported, with soft cushioned neoprene, rubber and even compressed air. They also have a leash attachment and handle for security. They tend to ride up a little during body-dragging and wipeouts, but far less now than they did in the past.

Modern waist harnesses can include a moulded outer shell, providing significant support and rigidity, as well as cost, to this type of harness. It is, however, your connection point to your engine and comfort that is key if you are kiting a lot or for long periods of time.

Both types of harness have a spreader bar across the front, fitted with the harness hook in the centre. This is made from stainless steel and is very strong. On modern waist harnesses this spreader bar is wrapped in foam and neoprene to prevent it rising up and digging into the pilot's ribs. When it comes to making a good choice, purpose and fit will be the main considerations: what will you be using it for and is it the right size? They range in price and colour, and cost between £100 and £200.

▲ Ready to go.   ▼ Checking the kite.

HELMETS

Mandatory for teaching, and strongly advisable for beginner to intermediate riding, helmets protect the head from bumps and knocks. Specific kiteboarding helmets today are lightweight and comfortable in design. Most have open ears to allow better hearing, and no peaks to allow the pilot to see the kite.

Helmets must display an approved safety standard certificate and be suitable for use in water; a motorcycle helmet is not appropriate. At the extremes, helmets are also commonplace at speed and slider competitions, which I will expand upon in the final chapter.

BUOYANCY AIDS AND IMPACT JACKETS

Like helmets, buoyancy aids are mandatory in the learning environment and must carry a certified safety mark identifying their buoyancy level. In Europe this is 'EN393', which means it carries 50 Newtons of buoyancy, which is generally regarded worldwide as a suitable flotation amount.

10 Newtons = 1kg of neutral buoyancy. It is estimated that an average person requires approximately 50 Newtons of buoyancy to enable adequate prolonged conscious flotation in water. A buoyancy aid will not, and is not designed to, float an unconscious person face up. A buoyancy aid will not help an unconscious casualty.

Impact jackets are thick neoprene jackets that fit very tightly and look like body armour from a distance. They are generally less buoyant (around 30 Newtons, which is why they are unsuitable for teaching beginners), but they are ideal for easing the transition towards not wearing a flotation jacket.I often give impact jackets to newly independent progressing intermediate kiteboarders to aid the transition from wearing a buoyancy aid to going without, especially when they are going into open sea and deep water for the first time. They have also become popular with freestylers and big-wave surfers alike as they help to protect against impact, and make you look more ripped!

BUYING YOUR OWN EQUIPMENT

Just like when you buy your first car, there are many kiteboarding brands out there to choose from, and models of kite within each manufacturer's range. In order to make a sensible decision, you need to consider a few things when choosing the right kit:

1. Where will you use it?
2. Do you live on a lake with flat water and light winds in the summer only, or do you live in an exposed coastal location with consistent and often strong trade winds through a season of the year?
3. What type of person are you? Are you big or small, tall or short?
4. Do you tend to be heavy on equipment, or do you take care of your belongings meticulously? There is no point investing in a fragile, high-performance raceboard then leaving it rolling around with building tools in a van, or storing it outside in the garden all year.
5. There are lots of suitable kites for your first-time purchase, and every stage beyond this. As your knowledge and skill within the sport grows, so will your ability to make the correct kit choice for your level.

TRANSPORTING KIT

Travelling with your kiteboarding equipment and experiencing different countries, climates and kiting spots both on and off the water is a large part of the sport. As the world gets smaller, with airlines making every corner of the globe more accessible to the adventurous traveller, kiteboarding remains a relatively portable sport and it is fairly easy to travel with your equipment for a reasonable cost. In fact, some airlines run by an avid kiteboarder may give you a kiteboarding sports bag for free on transatlantic flights!

The power of travel to advance your skills shouldn't be underestimated; your first Egyptian kiteboarding week with seven days of constant warm wind and water can progress your level more than a year of kiting at your local beach would. I have come across keen good-level intermediate kiteboarders who live in the cities of Europe with busy lives and jobs, who kiteboard in the same way as many Europeans ski. They rent equipment, go in the premium season to the right locations and ride every day in the sun for a few weeks, before returning to landlocked living. This alpine-type attitude towards the sport has been made possible by an increase in the number of seasonal flights at decreased prices, and this has helped to extend kiteboarding's reach inland to a whole new group of fit, enthusiastic cosmopolitan people.

Transporting your equipment is easy to do and there is a huge variety of wheelie luggage options to suit all board shapes and sizes. It is always advisable to read up on an airline's policy for sports equipment and excess luggage to avoid any nasty surprises when checking-in. The fact that boards are generally under 2m (6.5ft) in length makes it feasible to travel with a small amount of excess baggage both short- and long-haul. Something that can't be said for a modern-day SUP racer... You should also make sure you get a good insurance policy that covers you and your kit in case of mishap.

RULES OF THUMB

1. **Become sufficiently competent at kiteboarding safely and independently before buying any equipment. Never buy the kit before this time as you will only be tempted to use it before you are ready. Inexperience also hinders your ability to choose well, since you will never have felt how it actually feels to kiteboard.**

2. **Fix a reasonable budget. You have to spend money on kiteboarding initially, both on lessons and kit, but you don't have to spend thousands. If you use your money wisely and don't mind second-hand equipment, you can learn and get kitted out for as little as £1,000.**

3. **Learn about the types of kites and board by reading magazines, having a look at some websites and forums, and talking to your instructor. This information needs to be absorbed and taken with a pinch of salt as everyone will have preferences and personal opinions. However, if they all say to steer clear of a certain product then it's probably worth doing so. Generally, hybrid, all-rounder kites are the best first-time kites. The specific model, colour and brand should be your own decision, depending on what you like the look, and price, of.**

4. **Try to avoid equipment that is more than three or four years old, or second-hand kit that has had heavy use in the sun or commercial teaching environments as it could be past its best by this stage. Don't be tempted by a 'too good to be true' deal, such as one that includes two extras kites, a spare board, a harness and half a bar. If someone is giving things away there is usually a reason, sometimes old, hardly-used kit can look great but be completely unsuitable, or even dangerous, compared to better-designed modern equipment. EBay or kite forums often get blamed for these scenarios, but I think you can find good and bad deals through all the retail avenues and none are better or worse than each other. The real key is knowing what you're looking for and not being led astray. This is of course where your local shop or school can be of invaluable help, giving good honest advice and often offering a buyback scheme once you outgrow your first set of kit.**

PART 3

The Future

13

Kiteboarding
disciplines

Kiteboarding disciplines

Kiteboarding is a very diverse sport, which is part of its appeal for young and mature people of all different sizes, fitness levels and aspirations. The environments in which the sport can be enjoyed vary just as much, from warm, flat, serene lagoons to raging oceans with high and dangerous seas. Even mountainous alpine regions and lakes high above sea level are frequented by certain enthusiasts of the sport.

People's preferences within the sport lead them towards certain genres that suit their style, aspirations and physique best. For instance, a surfer wishing to enjoy the windy days will probably migrate towards a directional board, and frequent coastal locations, to add riding waves with the additional power of a kite to his skills repertoire. Likewise, a confident sailor or dinghy racer may be interested in course racing, slalom or even hydrofoiling as a more exciting and individual alternative to bigger boat racing, which allows more ease of travel and less reliance on a crew.

The latest discipline to evolve within kiteboarding is hydrofoils, which now have their own racing class and World Series. 'Foiling' is the latest most technical and extreme form of kite-racing, which is growing rapidly worldwide.

FREESTYLE
This is the largest discipline within kiteboarding as it encapsulates everyone riding a twin-tip, from cruising and trying the odd chop hop to throwing handle-passes and megaloops. Freestyle is just that, a free, expressive, fun-orientated discipline that is centred around leaving the water, performing a trick and landing again on your feet, hopefully. Around 99 per cent of freestyle happens on twin-tips, although I have seen junior youth racing World Champion Oliver Bridge jump and loop his course-racing board while waiting for the start sequence to commence.

People develop styles within this discipline that can then be sub-categorised, such as 'old school'. Mark Shinn, Franz Olry and Flash Austin, to name a few, personified this great fluid style that incorporates multiple spins, big-altitude smooth jumps, board-off spinning pirouettes and so on.

'New school', on the other hand, involves faster unhooking manoeuvres, led by pioneers Elliot Leboe and

▶ **A freestyle grab.**

Lou Waiman. An inseparable team in the late 1990s these talented riders performed wakeboarding-style tricks unhooked from the chickenloop at low altitude. These moves are aggressive and powerful and are often over before you have the chance to take it all in.

WAKESTYLE

This daredevil attitude has led to the modern-day wakestyle movement. The PKRA World Freestyle Tour in 2013 saw all its competitive riders wearing wakeboarding boot bindings with averagely longer boards than in previous years. The high-scoring moves often incorporate multiple handle-passes, kiteloops and extreme levels of flexibility, skill and courage. The average age of competitors on the PKRA circuit is late teens and early 20s; it is not uncommon to see wakeboarding-designed knee supports being worn by older riders who have pushed the limits beyond the tolerance of their joints...

A further sub-category of wakestyle, which is defined by one event in Cape Hatteras (North Carolina) annually, is the Triple-S slider event. This unique format involves competitors using similar equipment to that of PKRA competitors negotiating their way over plastic obstacles, which can project them into the air (kickers) or cause them to slide along with style (sliders). This involves a very high level of both balance and skill and demonstrates a great crossover fusion between kiteboarding and wakeboarding.

▼ **Wakestyle.**

▶ **Untooled wakestyle.**

WAVERIDING

Riding waves is the passion and aspiration of almost all watersports enthusiasts, and in recent years it has been pushed to such extreme limits it is almost unreal, with gladiator-type figures displaying immense levels of skill and courage to take on fierce life-threatening seas and ride monstrous-sized waves on the shores of Hawaii and western Europe.

Kiteboarding has begun to play in these arenas and immortalised a few heroes into the big-wave history books. Teahupo'o, the worlds 'heaviest' wave, has now been ridden several times by kiteboarders in the most extreme conditions. Jaws in Hawaii is kited by local big-wave legends when the winter swells arrive, adding into the circus of surf, tow, windsurf and SUP chargers already filling its line-up.

G-land and Lakey Peak in Indonesia (dedicated high-quality surf spots boasting perfect-shaped tube rides that have been the stars of decades of surfing magazine covers worldwide) are now frequented during the trade wind seasons by expert wavekiters searching for the ultimate surfing goal of getting in the barrel. Margaret River in Western Australia, One Eye in Mauritius, Mavericks in California, and Ponta Preta in the Cape Verde islands (to name but a few) are all prime wave locations that kiteboarders now frequent, alongside the existing surfing and windsurfing schemes.

These fearless heroes lead the growing directional waveriding discipline that can be seen around any bumpy kiteable coastline worldwide. On my local beach at home I have noticed the change with, dare I say it, some of the more mature regulars migrating on to strapped and non-strapped directional surfboards.

Riding a directional surfboard is easy to do and doesn't require waveriding prowess to begin with. In fact, the opposite is true and the best way to learn is to practise on flat water. It introduces the tack and gybe (every windsurfer's nemesis) for which the rider's feet have to be switched when the direction changes from port to starboard or vice versa. This takes a while to master but gybing especially is more achievable on a kiteboard than on a windsurfer, at planing speeds.

As the wave size and skill level have progressed, so has a whole freestyle strapless 'skateboard-esque' mini-genre for surfboard riders. This involves kick flips, jumps, airs and even strapless front and backwards loops. These are becoming very technical and skilful, yet don't generally carry the same knee-popping aggressive consequences of twin-tip freestyle moves.

▼ ▶ **Waveriding.**

Big waveriding in the tube.

RACING

This discipline has really come of age since 2009. The current format of the IKA World Course Racing Championship has grown dramatically from an experimental group using surfboards in 2008 to complete the course, through a rapid change and expansion in fin and board size between 2009 and 2011, into the highly professional and regulated tour it has now become, with full-time professional riders, coaches and officials following it year round and worldwide.

The equipment now used is available from a number of competitive manufacturers and has to comply with stringent measurement and volumetric limitations, which are inspected before each event. Kites are regulated and submitted for entry in advance of the event, and inspected for their suitability, along with their control bar systems and line lengths.

The main format for racing currently is triangular or box windward-leeward course racing, for which racers cross the start line heading upwind towards the first mark, which they round on to a cross- or downwind leg. Courses tend to consist of two laps and last 15–30 minutes. The fleet can be as many as 50-strong in graded groups, making the start line an exciting place to be when the gun goes off.

The winner and subsequent finishers gain a certain number of points and these are totted up so that the person with the highest score can be crowned the event winner. Over a season, these points are added together in order to decide who should become the annual World Champion for both men, women, youths and masters.

Slalom, a sub-category of racing, has become popular in the last few seasons and is a fast and furious crosswind affair in which a smaller number of competitors race shorter courses in often strong winds. This is an exciting, nail-biting and occasionally hazardous discipline of racing, with competitors being very close together at high speeds. Most of the course racing professionals will compete in the slalom discipline as well at World Cup events, alongside course racing and, potentially, border cross.

BORDER CROSS

This is not a common format, but can be extremely fun to do and watch. It derives from alpine ski and snowboard races, for which obstacles are placed on the course – similar to a steeplechase in horse riding. These obstacles need to be negotiated by the racers without hitting them or each other and while maintaining their course and speed. A lot of space, and specific venues with flatter water, are required to lay the obstacles and course effectively, meaning it is quite a niche category.

LONG-DISTANCE RACING

The ability to cross oceans has long been a challenge to man, and there is an enduring desire to pit yourself against the elements and your own endurance. Kiteboarding has given this quest a new lease of life on an individual basis. Countless crossings, long-distance solo trips and longer-distance races have been attempted and are regular annual events, some of which I mentioned in the first section of the book. Newer-style mass-participation events such as the Virgin Kitesurfing Armada can attract up to 500 participants to do a coastal downwinder, in teams, for charity. This type of event personifies the positive attitude within kiteboarding today, and the 'stoke' for simply getting out there and being part of a great event for a good cause.

The inter-island HiHo event in the Caribbean, the Mondial du Vent in France and the Lighthouse to Leighton in Perth, Western Australia, also reinforce this sentiment all around the globe, and accentuate kiteboarding's adventurous and long-distance potential. Racing events are really reaching into areas of the world that hasn't seen this type of competition before, which is fantastic for these cultures and places and can only serve to expand the sport.

HYDROFOILING

Inspired and possibly reignited by the San Francisco America's Cup yacht race in 2012–13, hydrofoils have re-emerged in kiteboarding and are now officially recognised as a class in their own right.

Hydrofoiling is nothing new, and an adventurous and pioneering few have been foiling for the last decade. The scene has really grown again in the last couple of seasons, however, with lots of professional racers on the tour lending their hand to a bit of 'foiling' and progressing this technical discipline. Foiling uses the same kites as conventional racing but in generally smaller sizes on a given day. It follows a similar racing format and scoring system to ordinary course racing, with slightly lower top speeds and incredible windward reaching angles.

The main feature of a hydrofoil is the fin; boards are simply there to provide the rider with a platform on which to stand. The fin, however, can be over 1m (3.3ft) in shaft length with changeable bottom fins for speed, control and performance. Once water flows over the bottom fins at a given rate, lift is created, opposing the downforce applied by the rider, and the board rises from the water and the bottom fin completely takes over. A skilled hydrofoiler can keep a stable equilibrium of downward force through the board, against the fin, equal to the upward lift force the bottom fin creates. This generates forwards motion and is very laminar and smooth as the bottom fin is operating beneath the surface where there is no air or turbulence. The angle of both the long shaft of the fin and the front-to-back fin elevation is critical in order to allow smooth sailing. Learning how to hydrofoil can be a character-building bucking-bronco type of ride, as manoeuvring the fin into the right position often results in some spectacular wipeouts.

Hydrofoil racing is almost surreal to watch, with riders seemingly floating across the ocean's surface, silently and gracefully planing through tacks without the fin slowing or descending at all when highest-level riders do it well.

▼ **Learning to foil can be tricky.**

SPEED KITING

Along with our obsession to conquer oceans, man has an age-old desire to go fast: faster than anyone else. To this end, we have to thank Frenchman Alex Caizergues for breaking the speed record back in 2008 by achieving 50.57 knots (93.54kph) and starting the ball rolling for kiteboarding competition disciplines to be recognised. Speed kiting is not only arguably the most extreme category of kiteboarding, but it is also probably the smallest. A handful of crazy Americans and Europeans visit custom-built speed courses around the world at consistently windy times of the year and try to squeeze a few more knots out of their bodies and equipment.

It takes incredibly specialist equipment and physical strength to go fast at this level, and the smallest of margins can be the difference between world records and horrendous wipeouts. The basic format is to hit a measured 500m (1,640ft) course as fast as you can and keep going past the finish post. The time taken is then calculated against the distance to provide a speed in knots.

KITING ON LAND

Wind- and sail-powered vessels on water were the very earliest forms of transportation around the globe, enabling new worlds to be discovered and visited long before diesel engines or aviation were even dreamed of. Since then, attempts to harness the wind on land have been made, but the use of land-based wind-powered craft has never really taken off in the same way as it has on the oceans and seas.

This is in part because land has far more obstacles and rough terrain, making wind power impractical on the majority of surfaces. In addition, other more reliable transport options, such as horses, dogs and reindeer in the days before engines became the norm, meant that there was no need to look to the wind for propulsion.

◄ **Kite buggying – an exhilarating form of the sport on land.**

However, in the right environment – large open spaces with minimal ground camber or obstacles – wind can provide a hugely efficient mode of transport that works in far less wind than would be required on water.

KITE BUGGYING

This sport has been around for several decades and can achieve speeds of over 40 knots in very light airs at an average intermediate level, making it quick to learn, and exhilarating. It involves a pilot sitting in a three-wheeled buggy that is low to the ground while a kite is flown to leeward of the vehicle, which is steered by the pilot's feet and creates very little friction. The steering can enable all points of sailing to be achieved including both fast tacking and gybing. It is the easiest introduction to moving with a traction kite and an ideal step from stationary traction kiting to whizzing around, without the added power requirement of water displacement resistance, or indeed the balance required for standing up. This means that the sport is brilliantly suitable for disabled people, and provides an exhilarating rush without the need for your legs if the steering is executed by hand.

Most commonly 4-line ram-air kites on handles are used for buggying as they enable the pilot to launch and land the kite independently without generating too much power. They also allow instant depower by pulling in the 'brake lines', which destroys the kite's aerodynamic flow without allowing it to fall straight away. Handles are fitted with leashes, sometimes referred to as 'kite killers', which allow the pilot ultimately to let go with both handles and completely kill the kite's power as it falls in control to the ground.

The buggies themselves come in a few forms and sizes, with sleek large-wheeled models that are long from front to back being used for racing and speed. Buggies with fat off-road tyres and a shorter frame can be used for bumpier ground and sand dunes, and resemble a dune buggy in appearance.

The skill with buggying is not to follow the kite in moments of power or slackness in the lines, as the negligible resistance in the wheels can let you run over your own lines after the kite has fallen from the sky. This can cause the lines to tangle in your axles and require you to re-rig the kite.

Buggying has an avid and dedicated following, especially in the northern UK where expansive beaches are revealed at low tide, providing the perfect platform. Buggy freestyle, although very niche and practised by only a handful of crazy brave people, is both extreme and impressive to watch, as are the wipeouts, with wheels, arms, legs and kites going in every conceivable direction.

MOUNTAIN BOARDING

Also called All-Terrain Boards (ATB), mountain boards can also be used for kite landboarding, which requires all the same skills as kiteboarding on the water. It is, however, easier to get going on ATBs due to the lack of displacement resistance, eg you don't sink on land, but simply slow to a standing stop.

▲ Ragnarok race.

Kite landboarding is also an ideal stepping-stone from traction kiting into motion and is a perfect way for youngsters to gain the skills of riding a board before being introduced to the more challenging water environment. Kite landboarding freestyle has now reached an incredible level with experts pulling off high-altitude, technical, unhooked manoeuvres.

SNOWKITING

As I mentioned in an earlier section, snowkiting is simply kiteboarding on a different surface medium: snow. The venues for snowkiting are not necessarily flat like the surface of the water, or most beaches (although of course some courses on frozen lakes and the like can be totally flat); they can also be three-dimensional, with hills and mountains that need to be navigated and traversed by competent riders. The jumping potential with snowkiting means that it verges on becoming paragliding at times, as professional snowkiters soar across valleys hundreds of metres above the ground for minutes at a time. This imbues snowkiting with high-adrenaline, and risk factors, which makes it one of the most extreme disciplines within kitesports.

Equipment can vary from completely standard kiteboarding LEI kites with normal all-round snowboards and skis, to depowerable foil kites with specific boards and skis designed for the extra stresses and different angles of riding that snowkiting dictates.

As with all alpine sports, experience and respect for the mountain environment are crucial for success and safety. Even the world's elite kiteboarding champions found it impossible to complete the Red Bull Ragnarok race course at Hardangervidda across open terrain one year because of the huge diversity in wind and the surface of the racecourse, instead leaving it to the local heroes to reign victorious in their familiar conditions.

Freestyle in the mountains is growing and developing as the sport matures and diversifies in this frozen-surface discipline. Videos and competitions bear witness to competitors negotiating jumps, sliding obstacles and executing technical and aggressive freestyle unhooked moves above this hard three-dimensional frozen surface.

SPEED KITING ON LAND

This is a relatively niche and recent crossover between paragliding and kiteboarding. It is an extreme downhill experience during which the pilot wears skis and uses a small ram-airfoil on very short lines, making it similar to a parachute, to create lift. The result is a fast descent that often involves prolonged airtime sections, which allow the pilot to adventure into areas no skier could contemplate. This was demonstrated in 2007 when the north face of the Eiger in Switzerland was descended in less than three minutes.

▲ **Snowkite freestyle.**

14

Competitions

Competitions

Since the late 1990s, competitions in kiteboarding have been hotly contested around the world, with a number of World Cup circuits and large sponsored events coming and going over these years. The main competition structure today consists of regional and national events within a kiteboarding nation, giving progressive access to the international, continental and world tour circuits. Points can be accrued on selected national events, which will count towards world rankings and entry.

TOUR CIRCUITS

PKRA

The Professional Kiteboard Riders Association (PKRA) is generally regarded as the world freestyle tour, with a number of events worldwide that can be followed by selected professional riders annually. Points are collected from each event with discard options that allow occasional absence and a bad day to be overlooked. An individual will be awarded the winner of each event. The points accrued are then combined over the season and the person with the most points is crowned the annual World Champion for that year.

The format on the PKRA is usually double elimination heats of between 8–15 minutes in duration with two or four riders per heat. Each trick is scored for its technicality, execution style and risk factor. The points are added to let a winner progress through to the next round.

Double elimination means there is a second, slightly harder way back into the final for a competitor who is knocked out in the first round.

The trend and style of this tour is right at the cutting edge of modern aggressive freestyle kiteboarding and new moves and riders are commonplace among this young and dynamic kiteboarding discipline.

Almost all the riders on the PKRA are now using wakeboard-style bindings, with unhooked handle-pass tricks being the high scoring moves.

KSP

The Kite Surf Pro (KSP) tour is the world waveriding tour. It visits some of the planet's most prestigious and challenging wave spots, such as Le Morne, or 'One Eye', in Mauritius. It pits riders against each other in two to four person heats, during which they are judged on the

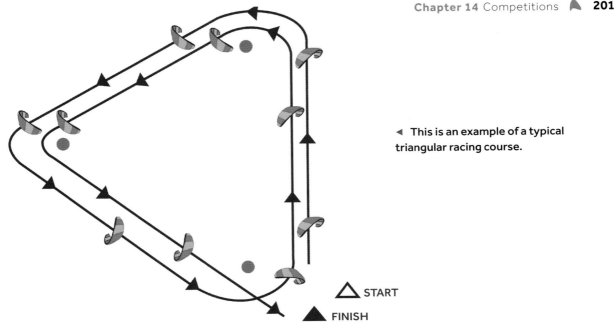

◀ **This is an example of a typical triangular racing course.**

△ START

▲ FINISH

waves they ride, their style, aggression and technicality and, in the most recent competitions, ability to get into the tube.

KTE

The Kitesurf Tour Europe (KTE) is a German-run continental competition circuit that was originally primarily based around freestyle but now includes a large racing fleet at specific events. The circuit involves three to five events across mainland Europe throughout the summer season. The events crown champions in men, ladies, juniors, youths and masters categories for single events and overall. This tour has been well supported and organised since 2010, with several hundred competitors at certain events and big-name sponsors providing backing. The tour is officially sanctioned by the IKA for both freestyle and racing. The ethos behind the tour is to provide a low-cost easy-access continental tour for the larger European kiteboarding market.

KTA

The Kiteboard Tour Asia (KTA) is the equivalent tour to the KTE for the Asian continent. Both the KTE and KTA feed into the world tours for freestyle and racing. The

KTA formed in 2008 and usually has five tour-event stops that make up the Asian continental tour from China to Indonesia and the Philippines. The disciplines include freestyle, and racing and twin-tip-class racing, which is a stepping-stone towards the formula series. The KTA has very much brought together Asian kiteboarding and heavily promotes participation for grass roots and kids through its 'kite kids' and event-training programmes.

Riders of all nationalities are welcome to compete on both of these continental tours, which promotes a real worldwide scope and enables travelling kiteboarders in the summer seasons of both regions to compete. The KTA is also officially sanctioned by the IKA for freestyle and racing disciplines.

THE TRIPLE-S INVITATIONAL

The Triple-S event in Cape Hatteras in North Carolina was established in 2004 and stands for 'Surf, Slicks and Sliders'. It is a unique three-discipline event incorporating wakeboard-style kickers and sliders arranged in a downwind run format to allow riders to hit a selection of the obstacles with their own style and incorporate wakestyle tricks. There is also a surf-style element as the location has a coastline with small waves and a large flat-water area inland of a coastal spit that extends several kilometres along the North Carolina coast. The event is hosted by a local kite shop and school and has become one of the coolest and most prestigious stand-alone events to win in recent years. It is regarded as being at the forefront of progressive wakestyle kiteboarding and all the top riders are invited to compete in this well-supported summertime event.

COMPETITIONS

Competitions can generally be segregated into three disciplines: freestyle and big air, waves and strapless freestyle, and racing.

FREESTYLE AND BIG AIR

This is the original kiteboarding genre, which is an expression category that has morphed and adapted over the years. Modern day big air and freestyle is almost revisiting the early days, when height and taking your board off were the order of the day. The biggest competitions are now big air, incorporating highly technical and consequential manoeuvres performed at altitude, often in very strong winds.

▼ ▶ **Modern wakestyle.**

This draws huge crowds and exposure. The Global Kitesports Assocation (GKA) runs the Freestyle World Tour, which includes both pure freestyle and some big air events with formats and judging criteria changing between them.

Perhaps the biggest event in the world for big air (and the ultimate crown to compete for), is the Red Bull King of the Air, which is now contested on the howling shores of Cape Town, South Africa. This event, which has a livestream similar to the World Surf League, attracts thousands of spectators as well as the cream of the world's elite, who fight for the elusive spots in the main comp through video entries and wild card ballots.

WAVES AND STRAPLESS FREESTYLE

The GKA also run the Wave & Strapless Freestyle World Tour, and more recently the Wingfoil World Tour. Waveriding takes these events to some of the most formidable wave spots on the planet like One Eye, Mauritius and Ponta Preta, Cape Verde to name only a couple. There is also a vibrant strapless freestyle discipline which allows no-wave days to be just as exciting.

RACING

Racing is run by the International Kiteboarding Association (IKA) who are affiliated with the Olympic racing movement and host World Championships, European and Regional Championships for juniors, youths and adults alike. There is a registered 'Formula Kite' class for Olympic pathway racing where the equipment is stringently monitored. There is also an unrestricted 'Gold Cup' fleet that allows any equipment. The first is to regulate equipment and costs for Olympic racing, the latter is designed to push development within equipment as the sport evolves and progresses.

The IKA formula course-racing and twin-tip competitions are run with a stringent set of rules that are overseen by World Sailing, the Olympic sailing class regulator. These are based on sailing racing rules, whereby the first past the post gains the majority of the points; second place gets slightly fewer and so on down the leader board. Event winners accrue points towards the overall championships throughout the year. There is a system of discarding an event result to allow occasional absence or bad luck to be disregarded. The point system is worked in such a way that it keeps the scores close, but rewards consistent victors.

Racing is now exclusively foil based for both Formula and Gold Cup, including youth and junior. Some fun twin-tip entry level racing still takes place to allow youngsters to gain skills and experience on the course before stepping onto foiling equipment. Twin-tip racing was the format choice for the first youth Olympics.

There are numerous stand-alone events all over the world from club get togethers at your local beach to high-profile large number distance races like Defi kite, where hundreds of kiteboarders race for miles along the Mediterranean coastline in howling winds.

Competitions are the shop window for the sport and are some of the most vibrant, colourful and exciting of all the sailing sports to watch, witness and enjoy all over the world.

Kiteboarding within the Olympic movement is making huge strides of professionalism for athletes, coaches, schooling and training, governance and interaction between nations across the globe.

I took great pleasure in helping the Australian and Turkish federations form and roll out their nation systems for training and schools. I believe it is healthy for nations to interact and share knowledge and structures to make the sport safer and more accessible. I have also enjoyed writing and allowing the international body to share good training syllabi and common practice for emerging and developing nations worldwide.

► **Kitefoil racing upwind.**

15

Governance

Governance

WS

World Sailing (WS), formerly known as the International Sailing Federation (ISAF), is the world governing body for the sport of sailing, officially recognised by the International Olympic Committee (IOC).

World Sailing is responsible for:

- Promoting the sport internationally
- Managing sailing at the Olympic and Paralympic Games
- Developing the Racing Rules of Sailing and regulations for all sailing competitions
- Training judges, umpires and other administrators
- Developing the sport around the world
- Representing sailors in all matters concerning the sport

GKA

The Global Kitesports Association (GKA) aims to represent the interests of the kitesports industry to support and promote the interests of all (professional) kite riders. The GKA works with the kitesport industry to provide reliable information about market developments and to provide riders with a platform to achieve the goals of the Association. The GKA's main objective, however, is to continually ensure that kitesurfing continues safe practice through the development and implementation of equipment standards.

IKA

The International Kiteboarding Association (IKA) is responsible for the central and joint management of five World Sailing International Kiteboarding Classes.

The activities of the IKA include:

- The promotion of kiteboarding internationally
- Holding a World Championship for each of the classes of kiteboarding
- Managing a World Ranking System for each of the classes
- Developing the Class Rules and Championship Rules
- Developing Equipment registration regulations
- Representing the riders in all matters concerning the sport
- Advocating on behalf of the sport with World Sailing
- The training of race officers, judges, umpires, measurers and other administrators
- The development of the sport around the world

IKO

The International Kiteboarding Organization (IKO) is a commercial training provider delivering certified courses for learning, teaching and instructor training worldwide. Formed in 2001 they have a worldwide network of schools and instructors and provide safe and quality courses. They are more dominant in developing countries where the national class association/governing entity is still evolving.

∏ATIONAL STRUCTURES

Since the temporary selection of kiteboard course racing at the 2012 Olympics, National sailing federations have been alerted to kiteboarding as an expanding and exciting class. With the inclusion of the sport in the 2024 Olympics, many nations are now integrating kiteboarding training structures and performance pathways into their current sailing programmes and federations.

I experienced this first-hand when I had the pleasure of helping the Turkish Yacht Federation (TYF) create their kiteboarding syllabus and nationally retrain their database of instructors. This was a hugely positive experience that proved that kiteboarding has been acknowledged as a serious sport and is a respectable career path in Turkey, both in terms of competing and teaching. This also means that learning the sport there is now safer and more structured, and competing up to international level is a reality for expert riders.

Numerous forward-thinking sailing federations, from Italy to Qatar and Australia, are introducing similar systems. British Kitesports Association (BKSA), Fédération Française de Voile (FFV), Kiteboarding Australia Limited (KAL) and many more take the role of national governance and management of the sport in their respective regions. Most National Class Associations (NCAs) sign up to the IKA to allow their national athletes to race and compete on the international and Olympic circuit. They also are now more commonly taking charge of training safety and beach access in their regions and sharing resources and best practice between one another.

The integration of these national systems under the IKA and WS umbrellas is allowing instructors and competitors to be accepted around the world more easily and pursue better career paths within kiteboarding as the sport grows and matures.

16

Taking it to a new level

Taking it to a new level

Alongside the expansion of the sport over the last decade and a half has come a thriving worldwide training and governance structure to introduce people into kitesports safely and positively. This has really been my domain, especially since 2004 when I became the Head of Training for the BKSA in the UK.

BECOMING AN INSTRUCTOR

It became apparent very quickly that kiteboarding required lessons if you were to learn safely and make any progress, especially with early equipment. Even today, with reliable modern depowerable kites, there is no real hope of assembling and launching a 4-line LEI kite correctly or safely without some form of guidance. This led to the formation of schemes by many of the leading national bodies around the world, and a number of commercial providers. The BKSA was the first and has led the way in training and safety for over two decades. It has helped the international bodies create frameworks for developing nations and has supported partner nations in creating their own schemes and cross-recognition of instructors. Most national schemes have a format for learning, becoming an instructor and progressing up a career path from basic instructor to examiner/training master. Most also have a school accreditation system for accredited centres to adhere to when delivering lessons to the public. These various systems are similar but different the world over and go from very structured and well-managed affairs in some regions to far more 'laissez-faire' arrangements in other places.

The interaction and cross-recognition of many of these schemes around the world is something I have become very involved with in recent years, and this progression is enabling instructors to travel around the world to teach kiteboarding wherever the wind is blowing through the trade wind summer or winter seasons, while transferring and upgrading their qualifications to the relevant region where they are teaching. The vision of a worldwide instructor passport is one that would permit an instructor to travel and collect regional credits for their competency ticket, thus legitimately allowing them to teach in lots of different countries. While there, the idea is that they could contribute to the regional management structure and follow a consistent scheme. Adopting and applying this global parity of standards and cooperative attitude is something kiteboarding can do better and sooner than any other watersport due to the nature of its modern and formative state, along with its unquestionable necessity for safe, high-quality guidance wherever it is being taught. This is obviously a big job and something I would describe as 'a work in progress' currently, which I believe will be expedited as we travel towards and beyond kiteboarding's debut in the Olympic Games.

▲ Directional coaching before hitting the water.

Obviously, in order to become an instructor, you need to be able to kiteboard yourself. Fortunately, learning the sport is a reasonably quick and super-fun experience, and it can take between three and ten days to master the basics. From there you can develop your skills and confidence until you feel ready to train to become an instructor. As with teaching anything, you don't have to be a World Champion to be able to instruct, but you must be confident, competent and able to lead a group effectively. The general level of kiteboarding required to become a Level 1 instructor is to be able to ride upwind in a range of locations and winds, jump in control, ride toeside and do a basic rotation in both directions.

Becoming an instructor is challenging and fun, and training usually consists of a week-long intensive course to educate you about: the scheme; how to teach; safety and managing risk; governance; and school management. At the end of the course it is common for a candidate to be given some shadow-teaching hours to help bed in their skills under the supervision of a qualified instructor.

Once qualified as a Level 1 instructor, you can teach four people with two kites as a maximum in almost all schemes. After a certain amount of teaching experience, you could consider moving up to the next level to become a senior or Level 2 instructor. This involves a further course to introduce more management skills, looking at the running of schools,

dealing with accidents, and higher-level teaching to build on the Level 1 skills already acquired.

It doesn't end here either, as an experienced senior instructor can continue to move up a professional career ladder to become an examiner or coach assessor. This last involves delivering instructor courses, inspecting schools, writing course materials and directing national structures.

With the evolution of foiling, racing and all other disciplines within the sport, instructors can now personalise and enhance their qualifications with foil endorsements, racing coach endorsements or become a specific advanced coach for waves, freestyle, etc, to add wingfoiling to their competencies. Therefore, every instructor's skillset is both unique and bespoke, providing diverse teaching opportunities for them and their customers, alongside variety within the job, thereby dramatically enhancing job retention and satisfaction.

Most national schemes have a national training manager or head of training, who will generally be a senior-level examiner, probably with varied watersports experience as well as hopefully being an organised person. As I have learnt, the paperwork often gets more extreme than most watersports at this level! The interaction of these different national training structures is becoming better and better as the world becomes smaller and kiteboarding matures under the umbrella of the IKA as its representative class for the Olympic discipline, and GKA safety with milestones like the ISO 21853.

The dream of teaching kiteboarding as a career, travelling the world and progressing up a structured career ladder is now a reality, with numerous people all over the globe relying on kiteboarding as a source of income.

◄ **Foil coaching perfection.**

me to see both young gap-year students looking for a ticket to ride and more mature career-change candidates successfully completing a course, then sending an email to thank me six months later from a beach in paradise as a competent employed kiteboarding instructor. This could be you in a short space of time.

IMPROVING YOUR PERFORMANCE: ADVANCED COACHING

Teaching doesn't simply stop once you have learned to go upwind or jump; in fact, this is where it gets really interesting. As mentioned above, the inclusion into the Paris 2024 Olympics has showered the world tour and athletes competing in it with professionally paid coaches, support staff, race directors and crew bringing highly developed and structured job opportunities in kiteboarding elite racing discipline. This is cascading down through squad and youth pathways nationally all over the world providing great coaching roles for seasoned and skilled kite instructors.

I have had the pleasure of helping to implement some of these structures and support the coaches and athletes in the UK, which has taken me outside my usual comfort zone and demonstrated what is capable when you support and push young talent correctly. I am very engaged and follow with eager interest the progress of our fab team and others I have met from nations around the world, and will be keenly following the action towards and during the games.

My more common coaching role is with intermediate kiteboarding clinics around the world, which I have been running since 2004. I find it one of the most rewarding and challenging parts of my eclectic job. The satisfaction of teaching at all levels provides a great buzz, and I think the ultimate example of this is seeing normal, everyday people landing their first backloop, riding their first wave or nailing their first tack. The stoke they genuinely feel and pass on to a group of similar people, makes for a wonderful environment to work in.

As this sector of the market grows and matures there will be more and more opportunities to race and train with

World Champions, ride waves with the gurus, learn to foil on all sorts of powered craft from kites to wings, eFoils to towed foils or even off the 'ladder' for self-propelled foils and perfect your style with freestyle legends. My advice to everyone at every level is to never stop learning or taking advice as we can all progress further, faster and higher with a little expert help.

THE INDUSTRY

Having worked within the watersports industry in the UK and around the world since 1994, I have seen trends, fads and recessions come and go. There are growing segments within the sport, most recently with the emergence of wingfoiling and foiling in general, all of which are expanding rapidly at the moment, along with their respective opportunity potential. The retail sector is often a starting point for people getting into the watersports or kiteboarding industries, and it is relatively easy to get a job working in your local shop or even for a distributor or brand as a rep or rider. This is how I cut my teeth for over a decade, working with windsurfing then kiteboarding brands at my local shop.

Competition circuits are now established, busy entities that require man- and woman-power for everything – from attending event sites, judging race direction, marshalling and water safety, social media, marketing, commentating and lots more. I speak to young and old colleagues alike who are busy travelling the world keeping these circuits running smoothly and having the time of their lives doing it.

The sport's training and governance is also expanding greatly, providing more and more career progression from teaching beginners through to becoming a national training manager.

The kiteboarding business is a multi-million-dollar global industry with endless opportunities in every sector and country. Many of the world's super-rich have dedicated teams on the superyachts discretely pushing the limits and their own experiences in some the most exclusive and inaccessible places on Earth. Despite its growth

and international stretch across the globe, kiteboarding somehow still remains a small and close-knit community, with everyone knowing everyone at events, conferences and annual functions. I have on countless occasions helped or met a fellow kiter on a remote bit of beach somewhere obscure, to then learn they spent the season with a close pal, or I personally taught them to be an instructor 15 years ago, and so on. Hence, it's always a good idea to move with respect between the manufacturers, associations and beyond, as reputation counts for a great deal.

THE FUTURE IS BRIGHT

I wrote a dissertation on kiteboarding in 2002 when it was still a somewhat unknown entity, and I said back then that kiteboarding is here to stay and will grow and blossom into a widely participated and respected sport. Over two decades later I can say that it was not a bad prediction, but what is to come now?

Kiteboarding *is* here to stay, although some people, manufacturers and schools come and go over the course of time, many of the people call friends and colleagues have made careers within the sport and have grown and evolved with it. I'm sure Dutotone, Cabrinha, North, F-One and all the others will still be great brands in another decade, but what will the sport be then? Will speedkiters be exceeding 100kph (62mph)? Will megaloops be 100m (328ft) high and kiters be rotating around their kites? Will everyone be riding some far greater variety of board types including foils?

It is safe if you follow the structured practices in place. It is reaching into cosmopolitan cities and landlocked regions with clubs and social groups gathering far from any kite spot to mix and chat, even though intensive, short-lived kiting holidays are their primary experiences of kiteboarding.

The increasing number of women and young people getting into kitesports is also a very positive sign of sustainability. I know several kiteboarding families who all kiteboard: Mum, Dad and all the kids. I have also had the pleasure of

▲ **Easyriders, mid downwinder stoke, Brazil.**

working and holidaying with the famous Bridge family over the years. With a World Champion mum, two sons on the World Tour for kiteboarding at some points in time, two of whom dominate their disciplines for freestyle and Olympic racing, and a highly successful kiteschool and shop in Devon, the water truly is a way of life for them.

Entrepreneurial social corporate events are being hosted worldwide for kiteboarding professionals to network, kiteboard and look at new business ideas through the medium of the sport. As a result, large new regions of trade wind-rich coastlines are seeing major economic growth and investment directly due to visiting kiteboarders like the NE coastline of Brazil, whose tourism is 95 per cent kiteboaring based for 500 miles of coastline, from Fortaleza to Atins.

True professional kiteboarding competitors travel the world following the vigorous tour schedules, as athletes with coaching and support staff on full-time salaries paid by sponsors and manufacturers, and these people are proper athletes who have to work extremely hard to get a break and maintain their performance levels.

Trainers and coaches such as myself are busier than ever before and work towards establishing worldwide training systems and interlinking structures that enable instructors to work, travel and progress within a sustainable industry. I have never known a more opportune time for kiteboarding and have to say I am excited about the next decade of being involved in this great sport and way of making a living.

I think it is fair to say kiteboarding has arrived. The question now is: where do you want it to take you?

► Jamaican bobsleigh fancy dress team in Brazil 2013: (from left to right) Amanda, Andy, Will and Tom.

INDEX

Andy Gratwick is a former Kite Racing Champion, and has been the Head of Training for the BKSA since 2006 and Head Coach for BSUPA since 2008. As ISAF's first kiteboarding technical expert, he wrote the syllabi for how kiteboarding should be taught for the UK, Australia, Turkey and the World Federation. He did the same for SUP and more recently for wingfoiling. Easyriders, his watersports school, has two centres in Sandbanks, Dorset, and also delivers worldwide coaching holidays.

ACKNOWLEDGEMENTS

This book would not have been possible without the help of family, friends and the fantastic team at Bloomsbury, as is always the case with a big project.

There are a few people who deserve special thanks, as without their help this may never have materialised. My wife Amanda for her tireless patience over photos and proofreading, along with Sarah Gale. Roger Turner, Will King and WS for their photos and willingness to get wet for them. My fantastic team at Easyriders and all our holiday guests for their willing/shameless modelling during the creation of this book.

PICTURE CREDITS

Adobe Stock: 2

Easyriders: 13, 22, 52, 53, 55, 61, 62, 63, 72, 84, 91, 92, 94, 97, 101, 102, 103, 105, 106, 107, 108, 109, 111, 115, 118, 121, 123, 124, 125, 132, 133, 136, 137, 151, 153, 154, 161, 165, 167, 168, 169, 171, 175, 184, 191, 202, 205, 214, 217

Flexifoil International Ltd: 16

Getty: 18, 21, 172

World Sailing: 59, 64, 65, 68, 70, 71, 76, 77, 78, 79, 95, 126, 127, 128, 129, 130, 131, 144, 145

North 158, 159

Roger Turner: 85, 86, 87, 81, 141, 134, 135

Shutterstock: 7, 9, 10, 15, 40, 49, 50, 56, 88, 110, 138, 146, 149, 192, 195, 196, 206